The Value Trail

The Value Trail *is a breath of fresh air in management literature. It gives excellent examples on how organizations should operate to survive in the current competitive landscape ensuring that customer value perceived is at the top of the pyramid.*
Albert Ros Manasanch, Supply Chain and S&OP Director, Wrigley Spain

A radical new approach to value creation. A breakthrough contribution to strategic management. In his new book, Dr Sansó combines his deep academic knowledge with his wide experience as strategic consultant to generate a new, comprehensive framework to understand and manage the true sources of competitiveness within firms. An innovative framework to be used by senior managers, but also a must for MBAs and graduate business students.
Xavier Ferràs, Dean, Faculty of Business & Communications,
Vic University (Barcelona); Visiting Professor, ESADE Business School

To Bernat, who came along with this book, and his mother.

The Value Trail

How to Effectively Understand, Deploy
and Monitor Successful Business Models

MARC SANSÓ

GOWER

Gower Applied Business Research
Our programme provides leaders, practitioners, scholars and researchers with thought provoking, cutting edge books that combine conceptual insights, interdisciplinary rigour and practical relevance in key areas of business and management.

Published by
Gower Publishing Limited
Wey Court East
Union Road
Farnham
Surrey, GU9 7PT
England

Gower Publishing Company
110 Cherry Street
Suite 3-1
Burlington, VT 05401-3818
USA

www.gowerpublishing.com

British Library Cataloguing in Publication Data
A catalogue record for this book is available from the British Library.

Library of Congress Cataloging-in-Publication Data
Sansó, Marc.
    The value trail : how to effectively understand, deploy and monitor successful business models / by Marc Sansó.
        pages cm
    Includes bibliographical references and index.
    ISBN 978-1-4724-5256-6 (hardback)—ISBN 978-1-4724-5257-3 (ebook)—ISBN 978-1-4724-5258-0 (epub) 1. Success in business. 2. Consumer satisfaction. 3. Branding (Marketing) I. Title.

    HF5386.S3237 2015
    658.4'012—dc23

                                                                          2014033762

ISBN 9781472452566 (hbk)
ISBN 9781472452573 (ebk—PDF)
ISBN 9781472452580 (ebk—ePUB)

Printed in the United Kingdom by Henry Ling Limited, at the Dorset Press, Dorchester, DT1 1HD

CONTENTS

LIST OF FIGURES

LIST OF CHARTS

LIST OF TABLES

PREFACE

According to the American Association of Advertising Agencies (2007), a typical American adult is exposed, on average, to around 600 advertisements per day in various forms. In 2012, the advertising expenditure of companies worldwide exceeded $450 billion (McKinsey & Company, 2012). In 2013, spam email accounted for an average of 77 percent of all email sent worldwide, and that was a downward trend (Cyren, 2014).

As consumers, we are completely overwhelmed—living in an environment in which supply massively outstrips demand. While companies keep on spending more and more money trying to grab our attention, firstly, and convince us to buy their products and stay with them, secondly, a central issue for most managers is how to capture customer insights and use them to deliver outstanding products and services that encompass an irresistible charm for the customer with a profitable business model.

In this harsh environment, value stands as the ultimate trade-off between customers and companies. The former expect value for their money, the latter are keen to be perceived as valuable. Today, far from old product-based approaches to competition, value propositions must be understood from the customer perspective.

The situation is the same for both start-ups and for big and consolidated companies—their value proposition must be critically assessed on a permanent basis. To do this, it is mandatory to fully understand how value is generated, transmitted through the entire business chain and perceived by the customer.

Understanding value involves considering it as an overarching element of the global process of strategic planning and deployment. From the grassroots of competitive analysis, which enables a deep understanding of business dynamics, to the definition of a brand new methodology to monitor company performance, over the creation of a solid competitive model, it's all about value.

So this is a book about competitive analysis, strategy planning and execution, yes—but, above everything, it's about how to become valuable.

Let us begin.

CHAPTER 1

APPROACHING COMPETITION

1.1 THREE STORIES

There are many clichés and misconceptions about business management. Myths that tell about leaders bound to succeed virtually from the cradle due to astonishingly intuitive business acumen, and companies touched by a magical wand. Clichés about a set of predefined rules about competition and success constituting a sort of shared conventional wisdom. Misconceptions that make us believe that this conventional wisdom is unchangeable and 100 percent reliable.

Real life, however, is pretty different: magical wands are very rare, and intuition is frequently wrong. In turn, there are other resources available that are precious to successful managers and practitioners alike and configure a completely different approach to competition. Thus, before we jump into discussing competitive strategy, let us reflect on these resources to create a necessary common ground for what is coming next. We shall do so through three brief stories.

1.1.1 Apple and Dell

In 1996, Apple was a very different company from the one we all know today. Moving from its past days of glory, and under the direction of Michael Splinder, first, and Gilbert Amelio, secondly, the company was immersed in a cost-cutting and somehow drifting strategy that caused a $69 million loss. Steve Jobs would completely reverse this situation some years later, implementing an aggressive shift back toward the foundational roots of the company. Although it would take some time, in 1997 Jobs drew up the framework for the Apple we know nowadays, announcing a $150 million-dollar investment from Microsoft which would allow the company to move back to producing its original core products. The controversy over the future of Apple, however, still remained the subject of debate.

Meanwhile, Dell was the solid new leader in the PC manufacturing business. Based on online selling, and through a disruptive strategy based on cost rationalization, value chain optimization and simplification, the company made its way to the top.

While the average research and development (R&D) expenditure was around 5 percent of sales for top PC manufacturing companies in early 1990s, Dell devoted less than 1 percent of its revenue to that purpose.

On October 6, 1997, at a Gartner Symposium in Orlando, when asked about how to address the issues of the then-troubled Apple Computer Co., Michael Dell, founder and CEO of Dell (and at that time one of the most praised and respected businessmen worldwide), said (Appleinsider, 2006): "What would I do? I'd shut it down and give the money back to the shareholders."

This was a few months after Steve Jobs's comeback, in July 1997. Though Jobs probably didn't like it very much at that time, he sure had the chance to have sweet revenge some years after. In 2006, when Apple's market capitalization overpassed Dell's (Chart 1.1), Jobs sent an email to all Apple employees (Appleinsider, 2006): "Team, it turned out that Michael Dell wasn't perfect at predicting the future. Based on today's stock market close, Apple is worth more than Dell. Stocks go up and down, and things may be different tomorrow, but I thought it was worth a moment of reflection today. Steve."

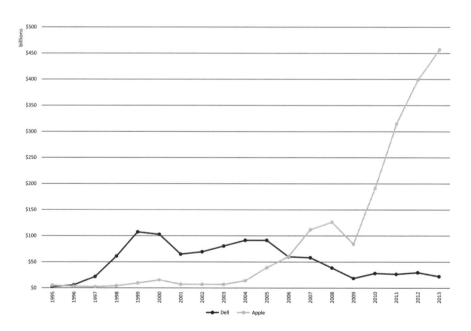

Chart 1.1   Apple versus Dell market capitalization (1995–2013)
Source: Data from Ycharts, 2013.

1.1.2 Leo Messi

This second story is about football and one of the most famous sports club worldwide, FC Barcelona. It's also about its main star: the four-time winner of the FIFA Player of the Year and captain of the Argentina national team Lionel (Leo) Messi.

In 2006, Juan Carlos Unzué (Futbol Club Barcelona's (FCB) goalkeepers' coach back then) noticed that a young Leo Messi, barely a freshman player on the FCB team, closely observed Ronaldinho and Deco while they were practicing free-kicks after everyday training (*Así se entrenó Messi*, 2012). When he asked Messi if he wanted to try himself, Leo replied, "Not yet" without removing his eyes from his teammates.

Six years later, during an interview given to Mexican newspaper *Record*, Leo Messi stated:

> *I am practicing free kicks after training every day. I had been told that mastering free kicks was a matter of practicing over and over again to acquire a good technique. They told me that I will find my way if I kept on practicing, and now I am scoring goals that years ago I didn't.*

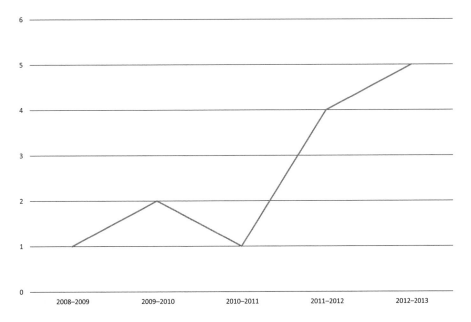

Chart 1.2   Free-kick goals scored by Leo Messi by season (2008–13)
Source: Data from Todos los Goles de Messi, 2013.

It certainly seemed that Leo's intense workout paid off. At least, this is what his statistics show—a significant improvement after 2011 summer (see Chart 1.2).

1.1.3 The Real Estate Bubble in Spain

On July 2, 2003, four years before the start of undoubtedly the worst recession in modern history in Spain, and while the signs of a real estate bubble where starting to be blatant, the Spanish newspaper *El País* published an interview (Aparicio, 2013) with some of the so-called most significant experts on the matter. Both Rodrigo Rato, Spanish Minister of Economy back then, and Jose Luis Estevez, Vice-President of the Spanish Valuation Society, denied any sign of what was about to come:

> *"There is no real estate bubble in the Spanish market, just a strong demand. This is, no doubt, a good moment to borrow money."* *(Rodrigo Rato)*

> *"House prices will never decrease, but just softly land towards stability. That is to say: there will be no bubble burst."* *(José Luis Estévez)*

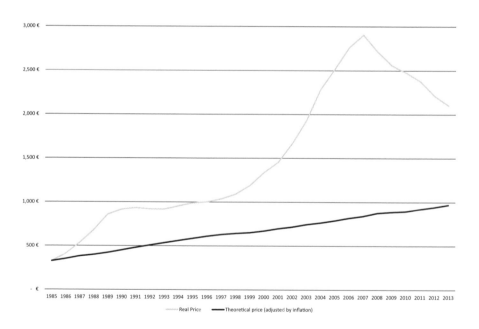

Chart 1.3   Evolution of average nominal price of houses in Spain (in €/m²)
Source: Data from Sociedad de Tasación, 2013.

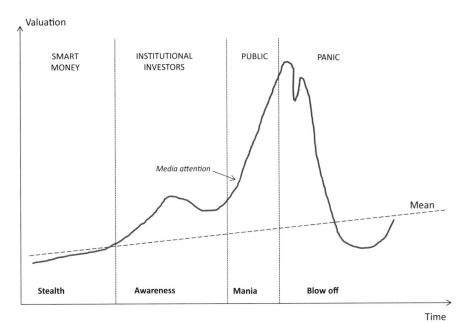

Chart 1.4   Stages of a speculative bubble
Source: Author's chart, based on Rodrigue, 2008.

Chart 1.3 reflects the evolution of housing prices in Spain from 1994 to 2014 (forecast). Take a look again and compare it with the classic stages of a speculative bubble depicted in Chart 1.4. Do you find any similarity? Awesome, isn't it? It certainly seems that, back in 2003, the Spanish real estate bubble was entering its public stage, and hence capturing the attention of the media (*El Pais* would probably agree on that). Now, assuming that both the Spanish Minister of Economy and the CEO of the Valuation Society in charge of assessing most housing transactions did have relevant information about price evolution and macroeconomic trends in Spain, and were also knowledgeable about the basics of speculative economics theory, we have to conclude that they were either consciously lying or trying to shape reality according to their previous assumptions.

1.2 EPILOGUE AND TAKEAWAYS

Each one of these stories teaches us a lesson about some of the most important pillars concerning strategic analysis and competition in itself.

The first story tells us about *the* difference between an opinion and an analysis (even for a respected businessman). Although highly overrated, an opinion is basically a statement with no solid basis and it is dangerous to use it as a substitute for a planned strategy. In the aforementioned example, Michael Dell basically predicted a dull future for Apple from the compromised situation it was in at the time. Besides, he was definitely influenced by the self-indulgence of Dell's dominant position at the time and did not take into consideration the viability of the fresh turn in Apple's strategy. Exchanging opinions is funny and definitely an enriching experience but will never be able to substitute a solid, fact-based strategy. Think about it: imagine that you are planning to invest in art and seeking professional advice. Would you rather base your decision on a one-minute chat with an apparent connoisseur, or gather as much information from as many sources as possible?

Remember: know the difference between opinion and analysis. An opinion is for a chat over a coffee, not for business purposes.

The second story tells us about the importance of practice over talent. Talent is important but extremely overestimated from an overall perspective and absolutely useless without proper execution. Identifying specific improvement areas and working on them are the basis for future success. If Leo Messi, probably the best football player of all time, advocates a continuous improvement perspective to critically assess his performance, we should all be applying it. The identification of these improvement areas should be based on a thoughtful and step-by-step analysis that envisions both business and company-level indicators.

Remember: success is very rarely achieved in first instance. Persistence and hard work are key to achieving results.

The third story makes us think about *the convenience of questioning conventional wisdom* to transcend everyday reality and gain focus on the real challenges we should be tackling. Only from an enriched, inclusive perspective will we be able to zoom out to get the big picture of the situation, whether this is an economy report or a threat assessment of our current competitive position. The game theory suggests that all good strategy should include an evaluation of the incentives for all players to behave the way they do, and, accordingly, a later adaptation of our next movements.

A proper approach to competition (as summarized in Figure 1.1), therefore, requires solid strategic planning to overcome our day-to-day routine, consolidate future plans, maximize our chances of success and should be based on something solid and traceable enough that allows further processes of revision and mistake identification. This definitely requires moving from the world of ideas to the ruthless battleground, or, in other words, looking for continuous improvement to translate what is planned into concrete terms. Having a solid strategy won't prevent your business from failing—you may want to think of it as learning how traffic lights work: crossing the street when the light is green does not guarantee that you won't be run over by a car, but doing it randomly may eventually kill you.

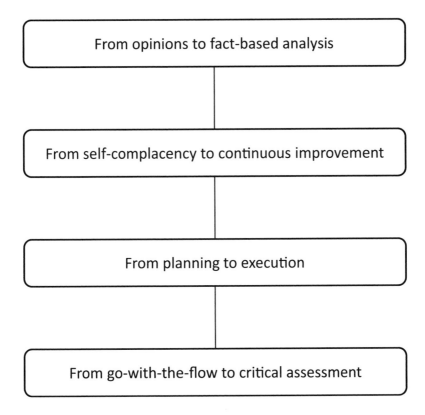

Figure 1.1   The approach for competition

These initial requirements will help us configure a conceptual path toward successful business competition. This path is divided into three main stages, which will be covered in the following chapters:

1. *Strategic planning and analysis* to understand, on one hand, the competition rules and the different business agents, together with the dominant value propositions and the potential drivers of growth, and, on the other hand, the differential capabilities of your company.
2. *Strategy deployment and execution*, to define a set of coherent corporate goals and to understand the available tools to reach them—aligning all existing resources within the company and accurately defining the actions to be taken, while creating a solid, winning culture along the way.
3. *Monitoring and reassessment*, to move from an intuition-based to a data-driven, market-focused organization—a process to make strategy accountable and to create a model which ensures efficiency and verifies customer attractiveness.

CHAPTER 2

THE ANALYTICAL PROCESS: AN OVERVIEW

2.1 AN INITIAL APPROACH TO BUSINESS

You don't start building a house from the roof, and neither do you start planning your strategy without having solid foundations. To start discussing what foundations are here, let's take one step back and think about how we usually conceive business.

As depicted in Figure 2.1, the most frequent way of approaching a business starts with the idea for a new product or service (stage 1). This is a so-called offer-focused approach (that is to say, its gravity center and trigger is the product or service itself) and as we move on we'll try to explain why this is essentially risky. Of course, every newborn product is conceived to be a winner. The problem is that the winning condition is not an inherent feature of the product, but determined exclusively by our customer, and, consequently, it would be much smarter to start framing our value proposition in that direction. Be that as it may, the obviously exciting thought of having a disruptive product or service, born to conquer the market (and make us rich along the way), is followed by the necessity of creating a company to support our go-to-market process (stage 2). We therefore start the functional design of our company. This typically starts by dimensioning the processes required to ensure the production of the product or service: inbound/outbound logistics, manufacturing and procurement, immediately followed by an accurate description of product features and characteristics that eventually leads us to a first draft of other functional areas (note how this all cascades down from the product concept). Pricing is usually addressed at this stage and thus it's normally based (at least as an initial approach) on two main criteria: *forecasted costs* and *desired revenues* (note how we consciously use the term desired and not estimated). Precisely the price determination process is the very first thing that tears us apart from our beloved product and reminds us of the need for something uncomfortable, unknown and feared: the *customer* (stage 3). Approaching the customer at this point is pretty weird and normally disappointing, mainly for two reasons:

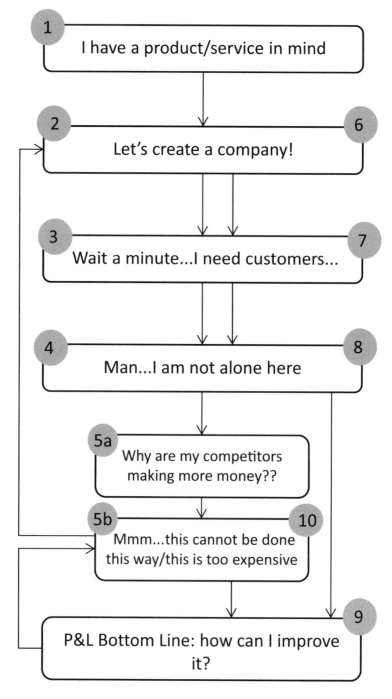

Figure 2.1   The traditional conceptual approach for business

1. We have all been trained to deal with product issues, which are normally far more predictable, objective and static than people's issues. Our mind, training and education are essentially offer-based, so we'll need to make an extra effort to reset it and start over.
2. Looking for customers for a finished product is like drifting around a giant puzzle trying to find a hole to fit your piece in. Up to this point we've tried to create something that we think is good, necessary and intrinsically valuable: checking whether the rest of the world thinks the same might be painful.

The act of looking for customers drives us from the comfortable boundaries of our company to a much broader environment, which will prove to be hazardous: the market. We normally call it market to mean aggregate demand, but it would be more accurate to call it business. We'll go deeper into the business concept in the next chapter, but right now let's define it *as a competitive playing field in which all agents involved in the flow of value creation are taking part* (stage 4). This is the point in which, inevitably, our new-born company and product are confronted with real life, and two certainties emerge (stages 5a, 5b):

- We are not the only competitor in the business. Other people are trying to either reach our same target (indirect competitors) or offer a similar product (direct competitors). From now on, all our offer-based metrics, ideas and indicators will no longer be based on an absolute scale, but relative. That is to say: it will be confronted with other value propositions and ruthlessly judged (or even dismissed). In view of that, we start thinking that maybe it would have been a good idea to take a look at the business environment before attempting any product definition.
- Some of our operational processes (procurement, distribution, product manufacturing, even recruiting) are either too expensive or it is simply impossible to deploy them in the way they were designed. This might be caused by multiple reasons, including competitive and operational criteria (the distribution channel is closed, there's no such supplier within my area of influence, prices of my competitors are significantly lower than mine, there are no available retail stores in the area, among many other examples), and this assuming that the legal and bureaucratic requirements are met.

Stages 5a and 5b act as living feedback (or a reality bite), eventually forcing us to move back to stages 2, 3 and 4 (now stages 6, 7 and 8) and rethink not only our internal processes and functional design, but also the core of our value proposition and core competences: it turns out that we were not as fantastic as we thought we were, or at least there's someone out there a bit more fantastic than us. This will be, needless to say, expensive and will also impact our payback and time-to-market, hence allowing new potential entrants to come and eat our piece of cake (market share) or the consolidated competitors to adopt new defensive positions.

Once our re-dimensioning process is done, we will finally be launching our product or service, will start competing and will eventually find ourselves looking at the bottom line of our profit and loss (P&L) account (profitability). As this is basically a measure of the amount of money we are taking home, we will definitely want to improve it (stage 9), so we may be tempted to go back to stage 5b (now 10) and rethink any specific area or process within our operating roadmap where we can cut costs. This will trigger a never-ending loop between stages 9 and 10 in pursuit of continuous improvement. Now, is this operating efficiency necessary? It most definitely is. But is it sufficient? Not by any means. In fact, this can be very dangerous as it may lead us to what Kim and Mauborgne (2005) *called a red ocean*: a competitive scenario which fosters competition based in conventional models and in which our unique driver of competitiveness is eventually cost optimization (in contrast with a blue ocean, that in which a unique value proposition is facing no competition thanks to its disruptive approach). Let's have a short example to understand this theory properly.

Applied Example: The Restaurant

Imagine that you are planning to open a fast food restaurant in a business area of your hometown. There are plenty of people to be served at lunchtime, so it seems to be a potentially interesting business, even if a quick glimpse reveals quite a number of restaurants and bars already operating. You will surely notice that a lot of these restaurants are offering pretty similar lunch options (for example, from 12–2pm, menu or a la carte, and so on) typically from a limited number of different cuisines (let's say local, Italian and Japanese), with an accepted price range (10€–15€, let us assume). You'll be strongly tempted to take these operating rules for granted and open your restaurant based on the very same pattern, emphasizing other types of characteristics that, in your opinion, do make a difference: for example, better quality or an increased number of available dishes. Such bigger complexity will definitely increase your operating costs, but this is the price you have to pay for excellence (few new contenders accept a different positioning initially). If it all goes OK and you make money quickly, all further internal debate is postponed. In the case that you don't, and as the pressure on your margin grows, you will typically start thinking that lowering your average price is the only way to keep your product attractive and to resist fierce competition (the very same competition you gladly entered into and contribute to reinforce by *meetooing*). To lower prices you have to cut costs, this is a hardly a secret, so that you start cutting here and there, painfully at the beginning (this superb type of bread, the genuine olive oil, the additional waitress that reduces waiting times for customers) and in an overtly aggressive way as times goes by. The final result is that you have managed to be exactly as bad as the rest of your competitors, with an extraordinarily similar price and operating model, and probably a similar level of loss: congratulations!

In the meantime, a new restaurant has opened its doors right next you. As you condescendingly observe the very first movements, you could predict a sure fiasco. However, it soon turns out to be doing pretty well. A quick look reveals a completely differential value proposition:

1. Instead of having the customers eating lunch at the restaurant, all dishes are ready-to-go and conceived to be consumed either at the office, or in public spaces throughout the city center. The required facilities are, therefore, much smaller and simpler than a traditional restaurant. This, combined with a minimum number of face-to-face employees, allows a serious reduction in the required capital expenditure, and therefore a direct impact on final price.
2. Online orders and scheduled pick up or free deliveries are available after customer registration. This not only provides a very much appreciated degree of adaptation and flexibility (no more queuing or rushing to get a seat), but also a deep understanding of customer insights, favorite dishes, peak hours and hot demand zones.
3. Among many other things, this also allows dishes with low uptake to be dismissed, focusing on highly profitable dishes and menus.
4. The combination of low prices, high volumes and profitable products is used to offer a blockbuster loyalty program based on heavy discounts that reinforces customer perception of value and secures future earnings.
5. Manufacturing (cooking) and inbound/outbound logistics (deliveries) are centralized. All fresh dishes are cooked and delivered on a daily basis, and hence the whole process is fully dimensioned for quick expansion throughout different city areas. In fact, it soon turns out that your new neighbor is basically a very successful pilot for a much more aggressive plan!

What is described above is, as you have probably already guessed, an existing and successful catering franchise, initially located in Barcelona (Catalonia): Nostrum. Founded in 1999, Nostrum opened its first restaurant in the Eixample district of Barcelona (see Chart 2.1), specifically targeting those customers looking for traditional and quality-based food. As this segment was severely impacted by the financial crisis, the company underwent major repositioning as a result of comprehensive analysis from a medium-term perspective, allowing a spectacular turnaround in 2012 and the rise of a new business model, namely *home meal replacement*. This disruptive approach offers a completely different value proposition, based on a set of simple key concepts:

1. Expensive or self-cooked meals are for leisure time. Lunch on working days is an obligation.
2. The offering is neither quality food nor a relaxing moment. It is time and money saving.

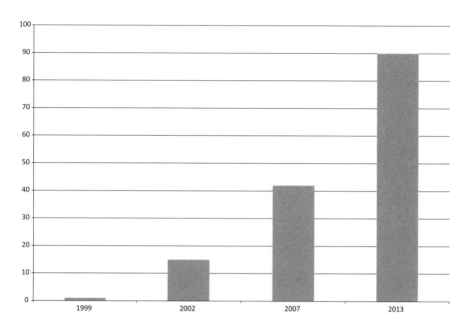

Chart 2.1   Number of Nostrum restaurants
Source: Data from Nostrum.eu, 2013.

3. The competitive drivers are price, flexibility and service, compared to traditional quality and service.
4. The centralized operating framework allows the creation of scale economies and the further development of a profitable franchise model.

The case of Nostrum is a very interesting example of how taking the challenge of questioning conventional wisdom and rethinking all competition rules for a specific business is the first step toward success. In fact, it's a good example of how a solid strategic analysis should be framed differently than the process depicted in Figure 2.1 (which potentially grants the aforementioned lame results). Let's try to conceptualize it.

2.2 A MUCH BETTER APPROACH

The very first (and probably the most important) difference between the flow depicted in Figure 2.1, namely the *traditional way of approaching business* and the one in Figure 2.2, the *optimized way of approaching business* is the starting point. Chapters 2 and 3 reveal how dangerous commencing your analysis through the product or service idea (offer side) can be. Instead of that, we should be starting from the demand side. The key matter is not, what should I be selling?

It is, what specific need should I be meeting? The answer to this question won't be found around the product itself, no matter how many changes in its features we introduce or how awesome we think it is. It's the customer who we should be paying attention to first, as it all starts with him. The customer is the source of money, which he will gladly exchange for value. The product is the vehicle to deliver a bundled portion of value, a package made out of very different things such as brand, a service layer, or tangible and intangible product features. Instead of sending successive packages to different customers in hope of lucky and uncertain matchmaking, it does seem smarter to approach a specific customer addressing an unmet need or a poorly covered one (stage 1 in Figure 2.2) to further deliver the right product or service to satisfy it.

Therefore, approaching the demand side should be the trigger for all business projects. Assessing the demand requirements equals analyzing a complex environment conformed by different agents (stage 2) that requires a comprehensive, step-by-step guided process to apprehend drivers of success (stage 3). Thus, this environment is basically conformed by *customers* (stage 3b), with specific insights regarding their purchasing processes in regards of a given set of value propositions brought in by different *competitors* (stage 3a) and deeply influenced by *other agents* (stage 3c: distributors, suppliers, retailers, prescribers, among others). From now on, we shall refer to this environment as the *business* itself.

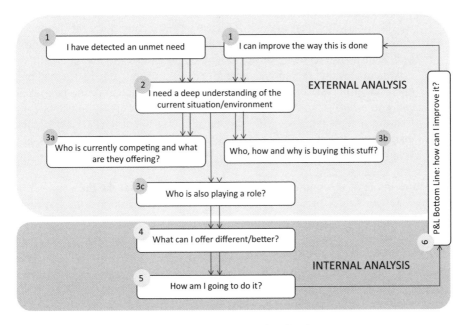

Figure 2.2   The optimized way of approaching business

At this point, we should have a clear perspective of our differential value proposition, *compared to the current ones* (stage 4). This is a concept to be highlighted, for the only way for our product or service to be successful is to be different in some way (cheaper, more innovative, faster, premium and so on), according to our core competences as a company. How we conceptualize and deploy this will be further developed in Chapter 4, but the foundations of this idea should be solid this far (remember the red ocean concept explained in Section 2.1).

Having this rigorous and deep understanding of what needs to be done to be successful in a given business, namely the drivers of competitiveness, and a solid idea of how can we offer a significant improvement or a differential value proposition, we are now ready to start thinking about how are we actually going to do it (stage 5). This process is partially described in Section 2.1, while assessing the go-to-market strategy for our company. However, there are two key differences with the process described in Figure 2.1:

1. The functional design and operating model of our company is not built around the product, but around the value proposition in regards of the drivers of competitiveness. This is built upon the analysis of the business requirements (customer + competitors + other agents) and the capacities of our business model (what we can do significantly better than our competitors). We will be reviewing how to do this in Chapters 3 and 4.
2. The continuous improvement process in our operating model is also a must. However, and despite the bottom line of our P&L account, this is something we should always keep an eye on (stage 6), the benchmark for this feedback shouldn't be only the product itself, but the changes in customer insights (a diminished purchasing power, a new target and so on) and competitive drivers (a new and disruptive value proposition). Confronted with that, our operating processes and expenses should be both efficient (costs measured and controlled) and effective (costs and resources properly allocated). In Chapter 5, however, we will see that all these metrics (P&L, customer insights, competitive drivers and internal processes) and indicators are deeply interrelated.

A good example of this could be the compelling situation that the then-new CEO of Lego, Jørgen Knudstorp, had to face in 2004, when he assumed the position. Let's examine it.

Applied Example: LEGOLAND

As shown in Chart 2.2, in 2004 LEGO was facing a dual challenge: the combination of declining incomes and high operating leverage (salience of fixed costs) was rapidly bringing the company to bankruptcy.

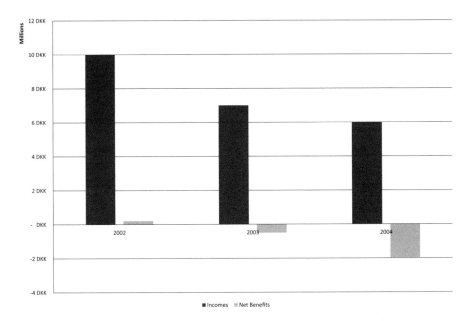

Chart 2.2   Key P&L figures for Lego (2002–4)

Source: Data from Lego Group Annual Reports, 2002–4.

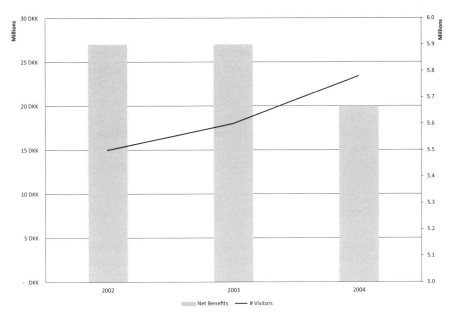

Chart 2.3   LEGOLAND parks aggregate figures (2002–4)

Source: Data from Lego Group Annual Reports 2002–4.

Given this situation, and in the middle of a ruthless war with low-cost competitors, Knudstorp was probably tempted to attempt a dramatic cost-cutting process right away that would indiscriminately affect all divisions and processes. Instead of that, he pushed through a complete strategic revision of the value proposition, core competences and operating model of the company called Shared Vision.

At that time, LEGOLAND, the chain of Lego-themed parks, consisted of four different parks located in Europe (Denmark, England and Germany) and the United States (Florida). The German park, in fact, had opened its doors less than two years ago. The evolution of key figures for these parks, depicted in Chart 2.3, showed a 26 percent decline in net benefits in 2004 combined with a sustained increase in visitor numbers. This typically reflects an inefficient situation in terms of operating model, hence turning the parks into perfect candidates for closure given the situation described above.

Meanwhile, the outcomes of the Shared Vision program stated that the Lego brand was leveraged by different key competitive assets that pretty much differentiated the company from its low-cost competitors and hence should be the basis for a future recovery. There were three core assets: the *Lego brick* itself, easily recognized and much appreciated; the *construction system*, as a platform for innovation; and the *loyalty of the Lego community*, based on an educational perspective of children's development and fun, passed on by each generation to the next one.

Knudstorp, despite the pressures and the critical situation reflected by the P&L account, and coherently with the outcomes of the analysis, considered that the LEGOLAND parks stood as a key vehicle to deliver the Lego experience, and therefore a product to preserve from any cost-cutting process as far as possible. Although the control of 70 percent of the LEGOLAND parks was sold for $460 million to the Blackstone Group of New York (while the remaining 30 percent is still held by Lego Group) in 2005, the essence of the Lego experience and the amount of resources invested never declined. This type of conclusion, from the mere offer-focused angle, would never have been reached.

2.3 THE STRATEGIC ANALYSIS GUIDELINES

Based on the conceptual flow depicted in Figure 2.2, we are now able to structure the overall guidelines for strategic analysis, which we will divide in two main blocks, to be tackled in the order specified:

1. An initial block for *external analysis* will address the challenges related to the business itself, and therefore everything related to the understanding of the underlying customer's needs, the relationship between the different agents,

the *drivers of competitiveness* and key factors to successfully take part in the business. This includes stages 1 to 3c in Figure 2.2.

2. A second block for *internal analysis* will assess the creation of value within the company boundaries, the corporate levers to enhance value generation and, all in all, the *corporate goals* of the company with regards to the drivers of competitiveness identified in the external analysis block. All these factors will finally converge in the creation of a competitive model. This includes stages 4 and 5 in Figure 2.2.

Stage 6 stands as the link between both analyses, the uninterrupted process of feedback considering both demand-side and offer-side metrics to validate the outcome of our strategy. Table 2.1 summarizes all this information, including a reference to the chapter in this book where it is specifically developed.

Table 2.1   Overview of the strategic analysis process

Block	Framework	Elements of analysis	Expected outcomes	Related chapter
External Analysis	Business	• Competitors • Customers • Agents of value (suppliers, distributors, retailers, and so on) • Value flow: Appreciation, Concentration and Predation	• Drivers of competitiveness • Key success factors	Chapter 3
Internal Analysis	Company	• Internal processes • Organizational design • Know-how and core assets	• Competitive positioning • Levers of internal value generation • Corporate goals	Chapter 4
Feedback	Global	• P&L account profitability metrics • Market metrics • Optimization of operating metrics	• Key performance metrics and indicators • Changes in short and medium-term tactics	Chapter 5

2.4 KEY TAKEAWAYS

- The common way of approaching business is product-based. This starts with the product/service definition to subsequently build a company definition around it.
- This offer-focused perspective is risky and potentially not very profitable, given its natural drift toward a so-called red ocean: a competitive scenario based on conventional wisdom, small margins and cost optimization.
- Customers don't buy products but solutions for a specific need. The right way of approaching business should start with the identification of a customer need (demand-focused approach) to further develop an own value proposition to meet it.
- Customer needs cannot be assessed from an isolated perspective. Customers develop insights and purchasing attitudes as a result of the assessment of different value propositions (competitors), influenced by diverse agents (distributors, retailers, suppliers and so on) and other competitive criteria. This complex environment is called business.
- The only way a value proposition can become successful is to be different in some way. Repeating or copying other products or services eventually leads to a cost-based competition model.
- Considering the abovementioned facts, a strategic analysis should start with an assessment of the business requirements (external analysis), followed by an analysis of the company competences (internal analysis).
- The expected outcome of the external analysis is a deep understanding of the drivers of competitiveness of a business: how to compete successfully.
- The expected outcome of the internal analysis is an assessment of the overarching goals of the company with regards to these drivers, as well as the planning and deployment of the corporate levers to achieve them: what is the company able to do significantly better than any competitor?
- The profitability metrics of the P&L account, combined with a sustained measurement and control of other market and operating key performance indicators (KPIs), should be considered as feedback and a link between the external and internal analysis.

CHAPTER 3

OUT THERE AND BACK:
BUSINESS AND ENVIRONMENT

3.1 APPROACH

As mentioned in Section 2.1, a business is a complex environment made up of different agents that play a specific role. Throughout this chapter, we'll learn how to identify the competitive drivers arising from the diverse ecosystem of relationships existing between them, as well as understand how these relationships decisively condition our customer's perception of value. But this will be a bit further ahead.

First and foremost, we need to go deep down into the concept of business and establish a way to conceptualize it that enables a further analysis.

Applied Example: Surfing in Australia

Australia is a wonderful country known for many reasons, the sport of surfing definitely being one of them. Indeed, Australia is renowned as one of the world's premier surfing destinations due to its never-ending coastline, orography and privileged weather. In 2011, more than 2.5 million recreational surfers enjoyed this sport on the Australian beaches (Surfing Australia, 2011). This represents a massive flow of money and therefore a huge interest from a lot of people who wish to get some of it. In the long run, this generates a complex ecosystem of interconnected agents. Each one of them plays a specific role in the Australian surfing ecosystem, based on a given specialization that contributes to enhance it as a whole. Figure 3.1 poses an approach to it:

1. In the very center of the ecosystem we may want to position the *surfboard manufacturers*, like DMS or Clearwater. They significantly contribute to interconnect different agents, given their central position.
2. Surfboards are made of a combination of advanced materials that guarantees their buoyancy, aerodynamic features and resistance. *R&D centers in advanced materials*, such as ARNAM, work hard on the development of said materials, such as Expanded Polystyrene (EPS).

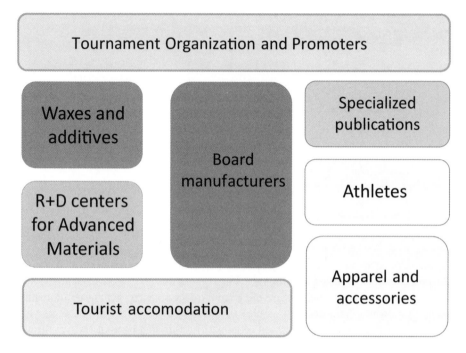

Figure 3.1   The Australian surfing business
Note: Illustrative, non-exhaustive.

3. *Wax* is critical to ensure a firm grip on the surfboard. Whether made out of natural components, like the one commercialized by Treehugger, or chemical additives, it play a key role when it comes to the surfer's experience.
4. *Professional surfers*, likewise, take part in professional *competitions*, such as Quicksilver Pro. The very best among them enjoy a star status and consequently play a major role in *specialized publications* such as tRACKs and *clothing and accessories brands* such as Billabong or Quicksilver.
5. Recreational surfers, for their part, not only consume the aforementioned products, but also require *tourist accommodation* (gladly managed by organizations like Tourism Australia) when practicing their favorite sport.

All these agents simultaneously take part and make up the so-called surf *business* in Australia. We will be focusing on the business analysis throughout this chapter but, before we make any further progress, it is crucial to understand the difference between three concepts typically misinterpreted and often used interchangeably: sector, market and business.

- The term *sector* refers to a group of agents who share a common activity and expertise in regards to what they produce (products or services). This is, therefore, an offer-side concept. The automotive sector, for example, refers to the group of original equipment manufacturers (the carmakers), and typically the first-tier suppliers. Note how they all share a common ground which is the car itself (or its parts).
- The term *market* refers to a group of agents (either final or trade customers) that share a common consumption or purchase of a product or service, for example the *senior population* or *pharmacies* as potential buyers of meds. More generically, this may refer to the unit that brings together said customers (typically a country, for example the *German market*). It is also very frequent to find the term market accompanied by the product of service that is consumed (for example, the *book market*) as an abstraction of the undefined group of agents that are supposed to consume it. Be that as it may, it should be a demand-side concept.
- The term *business* refers to a comprehensive approach to competition as a whole. We defined it in Chapter 2 as a *competitive playing field in which all agents involved in the flow of value creation are taking part*. The common ground for all these agents, therefore, is not the product or service offered (as there might be several involved) but precisely the aforementioned creation of value according to one or more customer groups (a segmented market). Note how the agents in a sector are aligned with a product or service, whereas in a business they are aligned with the economic flow derived from the creation of value.

The business analysis, therefore, allows an enriched perspective of the competition. Let's take up the Australian surf business example: speaking again of sectors, we could consider any of the shaded boxes depicted in Figure 3.1. The board manufacturers, the tourism agencies or the specialized publishers could be potential examples. Each one of them, taken separately, is made up of agents that share a common expertise on a specific manufactured product, service or activity. However, despite the sure quality of their surfboards, for example, this is not enough to explain the revenues of the Australian board makers. Which share of revenues is a result of having excellent beaches in Australia? Or outstanding touristic resorts? Or well-known champions? This influence is hardly quantifiable, but certainly undeniable. They all take part in the value creation, and therefore they are aligned with an economic flow from which they all benefit. Where is the value flow ending, and who is making its overall assessment? You guessed it right: the customer, our dear surfer. This is precisely what the external analysis is aiming to do: to understand the creation of value within a business by assessing the interaction between its players and the eventual impact on the customer. We shall refer to this process as the determination of the drivers of competiveness of the business. On the other hand, the conceptual interaction between the aforementioned players in regards of this value generation is known as the value chain of a business, and might be depicted through a graphic representation such as the one shown in Figure 3.1.[1]

So let's recapitulate: we have defined the framework (business) and the objectives (understand the drivers of competitiveness) for the external analysis. Now let's focus on the methodology to achieve them. To that end, we will be introducing the Three Dimensions of Value (TDV) model.

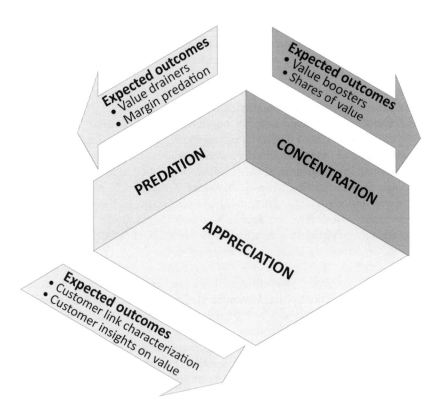

Figure 3.2   The Three Dimensions of Value (TDV) Model

---

1   In fact, the use of graphic representations of the value chain is strongly encouraged, as it has proved to be very useful to identify business players and their existing dynamics.

3.2 ANALYZING THE DRIVERS OF COMPETITIVENESS: THE TDV MODEL

The TDV model determines the drivers of competitiveness for a business by mapping the three most significant conditioning factors regarding value throughout the whole business. We shall call these factors *dimensions of value*, namely *Appreciation, Concentration* and *Predation*. For each one of them, we will be discussing its expected outcomes and analytical guidelines (Figure 3.2). These three dimensions will be a recurring element and a main thread running through the different chapters of the book, as they represent a fundamental concept which underpins the proposed strategic model of analysis.

3.2.1 Appreciation Dimension

The Appreciation dimension of value is the first one to be assessed, and it is primarily determined by the customer and the type of interaction we are having with him. It aims to answer two different questions:

1. What type of customer relationship is dominant?
2. What are the customer expectations and insights regarding what is valuable?

Speaking of the type of link that a company might have with their customers, we shall identify two different ones: the *transactional* and the *relational* link. We shall use two different examples to introduce the theory beyond them. Let's look at the first one to explain what a transactional link is.

Applied Example: The Airline Business

Imagine that we are analyzing the airline business to check how we can maximize the value delivered. If you try to replicate the customer insights regarding the purchasing process, you could come up with something like this (all data is fictional):

1. Online is, by far, the most salient distribution channel. Moreover, the purchase would be typically conducted through an aggregator site (edreams, orbitz or any other one among the thousands that exist), instead of accessing the airline site itself.
2. Available flight options are usually sorted and assessed on a price basis. Of course, other criteria such as number of scales, seat comfort or onboard services might also be considered, but only for flights above a certain duration. Let's consider that we have conducted an empirical research to understand the real value of these attributes for our customer and the outcomes are shown in Chart 3.1.

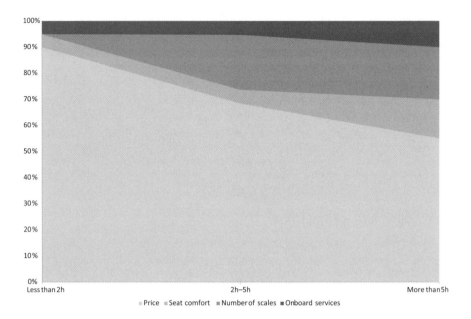

Chart 3.1   Perceived value of offered attributes, based on flight duration
Note: The data used is fictional and is not intended to be used for any purposes other than
assessment.

> The research indicates that price is always the most significant attribute, but its
> relative importance decreases as the flight duration goes up. Thus, whereas for
> flights of less than two hours, 90 percent of the perceived value is delivered by a
> low price, this percentage drops to 55 percent when it comes to the price of a flight
> of more than five hours, and it is partially substituted (in terms of importance) by
> having a direct flight, extra-comfortable seats or decent onboard services.

Based upon these conclusions, how could we maximize the value delivered as a
short-flights airline? It wouldn't really make much sense to invest our resources
in training an outstanding ground taskforce, enhancing meals or providing free
wifi onboard. Why? Well, because our customer wouldn't appreciate it. It would
be much better to invest our money in a cost-cutting strategy to reduce our prices.
Does this ring a bell with you? Yes: it's the basic approach of the low-cost airlines
competitive model.

Transactional links such as the one detailed in the abovementioned airline
example, are focused on the immediate and mere purchase of a good or service in
exchange of money, with no follow-up actions or loyalty-enhancing approach. As
a result of this, transactional links are price-based. The most significant share
of perceived value is delivered by reducing the price of the product or service,

as little more is appreciated. Try to think what you would give up regarding flight add-on benefits (seat, airport and so on) for a 75€ reduction in the final price of your Barcelona–Paris flight (1h and 40min) and you will understand what we mean by this. This basically takes place when comparing undifferentiated products or services (two products that are equally perceived), such as, for example, when buying aluminum foil at the supermarket and comparing the retailer brand with any other option. Note that there is no or very little aspirational or emotional criteria present here as it's a mere transaction. This pretty much reduces the choices to build a potentially successful value proposition to compete in the business, and is, in fact, risky. The reason is simple: reducing the available options for differentiation to a pure price competition forces us to permanently be the cheapest available option in order to be successful. As soon as another competitor grants a better price, all our customers will run away from us. And this is a very heavy burden to bear. On the other hand, a transactional business can potentially be as profitable as any other type: however tough the requirements, it's a matter of understanding the key success factors. Think of this: in every given business, one of the contenders (at least) is making money.

Relational links, in turn, *are* focused on the development of a long-term relationship with the customer. This relationship is based on the creation of a sustainable experience involving the customer himself, the company (and its assets, the brand being one of the most significant) and the purchasing process with its different stages (evaluation, purchasing, post-purchasing). We might conclude, therefore, that relational links are experience-based. By fostering relational links with its customers, companies transcend mere transactions, and hence obtain a competitive advantage based on their loyalty. This loyalty attitude partially shields the company from a harsh price-based competition which is the typical scenario for transactional links. Let's have a look at the second example to gain some focus on this concept.

Applied Example: Football

Imagine that we are analyzing the customer insights in the soccer business. Take an average Futbol Club Barcelona (FCB) member, for example. Members paid 177€ in 2013 for their annual membership fee. This fee is not a season pass to the FCB stadium, and does not grant them access to matches (match tickets are paid for separately). Barring some minor advantages, such as discounts on individual match tickets, official merchandising and FCB tours, the membership fee does not entitle them to any specific privileges. Thus, from the transactional process point of view (what they physically get in exchange for their money), the deal seems rather poor for the member. Imagine that the Real Madrid[2] (RM) commercial team, aware of this situation, contacts all FCB

---

2   For those readers unfamiliar with the details of European football, we should clarify that Real Madrid is Futbol Club Barcelona's historic arch-rival.

members to propose an irresistible offering: to change their FCB member status for a RM one with a 20 percent discount on their annual membership fee and free access to one RM match at the stadium. Would you imagine anyone accepting? Obviously not, and the reason is nowhere to be found from the transactional perspective (which is indeed better), but from the relational one: members are loyal to FCB, they have developed a relationship with the company/brand based on past experiences and underlying emotions (Figure 3.3 depicts this conceptual flow in five stages). Although a comprehensive approach of the process, and hence an accurate description of the value perceived by FCB fans, might be difficult to summarize, it probably has to do with both a sense of belonging passed on from their parents and a positive recognition of their past occasions of use: the emotion of live matches with friends, the joy of winning and so on. All in all, FCB can rest assured that is extremely unlikely that an average customer (member) abandons their membership to become a RM fan: even considering the poor membership benefits they are entitled to! Obviously, this kind of inelastic behavior proves invaluable for a company operating in any business, but the tricky part is that it does require a lot of investment and deep understanding of customer insights.

Note that, as mentioned, both types of links are potentially profitable. Understanding the concept of value for the customer is an essential way to start capturing the business drivers of the competition. Later on we will be discussing how to use this acquired information, but so far it is important to understand that it might be used to either reinforce current business dynamics or to challenge conventional procedures and create new value propositions.

So, to summarize, the Appreciation dimension of value for a business should provide a clear understanding of what is value for a business customer (*customer insights on value*) and through what different means it is delivered (*customer link characterization*). But how can we grasp what our customers have inside their minds?

Capturing Customer Insights
We have repeatedly referred to the understanding of customer insights as a key part of successfully deploying the model. However, we should look for *useful, sincere* and *applied* insights. How do we do this? Figure 3.4 gathers all the information about this process. The immediate answer is normally *asking* you customer, typically through surveys in their various modalities (online, phone-calling or face-to-face). Although sometimes convenient, unfortunately this simply proves to be insufficient. Not only because useful answers require the right questions to be asked, but simply because most of the answers are not either entirely sincere (let's face it) or a valid reflection of our customer's behavior in real-life situations. Imagine, for example, a commuter returning home after a hard day's work when somebody rushes up to him in the middle of the street introducing a brand new credit card and reciting a never-ending list of its advantages.

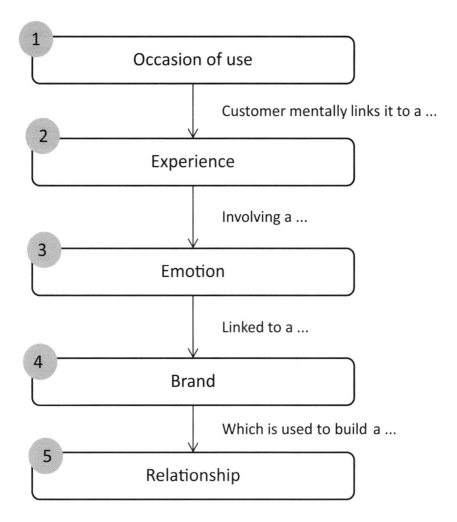

Figure 3.3   The relational link approach

Most of us would probably answer anything just to get rid of this person. And, even if the interviewee tries to be honest, some of the answers provided may not be useful enough to base a new business proposition on. If the interviewer, for example, recites a long list of apparently awesome benefits and afterwards inquires whether the customer would consider acquiring the credit card, the average person would be strongly conditioned to answer affirmatively (this is known as an *interviewer bias*). But… would this be a reliable predictor for market response? Try making this very same customer sign a purchase commitment right after his/her answer and you'll notice what happens. The same thing happens when it comes to questions themselves: not all of them are equally valid.

Getting back to the commuting example, imagine that we tackle our poor office worker on his way to work, and we ask him whether he would like to gain some free time and not be stuck in a traffic jam every single morning. Would he be willing to pay for it? Again, the answer is obvious, but useless. It would be much more efficient to ask him about the real value of an hour of free time, based on an accurate cost–benefit analysis and suitable alternatives. He may actually be fed up with traffic jams but he *wouldn't* give up a 5 percent of his monthly wage to avoid them. Well, not 5 percent but maybe 1 percent. Although just on Fridays. And only because, on Fridays, he gets to the office an hour earlier. But, just to be sure… do you think he would answer exactly the same if we contacted him online during the weekend, while he was comfortably leaning back on his couch at home? Probably not!

In conclusion, asking is necessary but simply not enough and, be that as it may, it is simply not a comprehensive approach to capturing customers' insights. We shall require a much more valid procedure: *experiencing* (Figure 3.4).

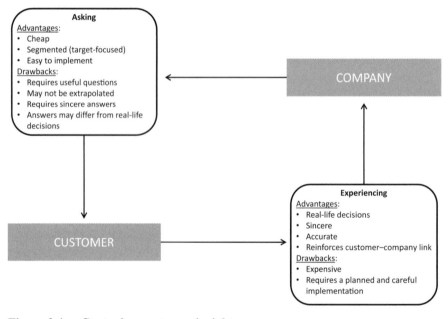

Figure 3.4   Capturing customer insights

Sharing an experience with your customer is a much more accurate way of capturing his/her insights on a specific purchasing offer. By this, we understand dimensioning a whole process to actually live a purchasing process with our customer throughout all its major stages, namely *awareness*, *consideration*, *preference*, *purchase*, *repurchase* (the so-called Purchase Funnel). There are many ways to implement this kind of methodology, but they all share two main characteristics.

First of all, they reduce the interviewer bias to the minimum by not *asking* questions, but *observing* customer's behaviors. Imagine that, instead of asking our customer about the desired appearance and attributes (price, type of fabric and so on) of a pair of trousers, we actually accompany him as he buys them. We could therefore capture interesting insights on the whole process, such as other purchasing options considered, specific time of the day in which he feels in the mood for shopping, the shop layout to optimize comfort and buying experience, total time invested, and much more. Another major source of information, of course, lies in the socialization of the purchasing process: the way our pool of customers interact with the brand or product. This generates valuable information for the company and reinforces the emotional link between it and their customers while reducing the interviewer bias (if properly done). This is why all companies struggle to have a strong presence on social networks today.

A second characteristic of these kinds of methodologies is that they naturally force the customer to descend from a theoretical level by substituting questions with actual, real choices. By forcing these types of situations, not only is the emotional link empowered again, but some undisclosed insights are revealed. It's not only a matter of sincerity: sometimes we are simply unaware of our reaction regarding a situation until we actually face it.

Imagine that we have recently started a bakery and we are planning to offer a brand new line of cakes targeting our frequent customers (we are planning to offer some discounts to reinforce cross-selling). We may not be sure whether the carrot cake, the blueberry cream cheese cake or the key lime pie would be more successful, and we just have budget enough for one of them. We could, of course, ask our customers about their preferences. This might be a good approach to actually decide the initial set of options, but, as we have already discussed, it won't be enough. Moving from *asking* to *experiencing*, we could actually cook all three cakes and offer them for free to all our customers for a specific period of time, observing the results. The conclusions, however, probably wouldn't be very useful, as it is much probable that all the cakes would eventually be eaten. This is because no real choice is made when something is given for free: we just take it all (this is typically what happens in an all-you-can-eat buffet: a lot of food is simply wasted). Instead of this, we could actually make some of our best customers pay a small amount of money (much below its market value) to actually have one big slice of cake. Just one, and just for the customers initially buying a specific product. Based on a sufficient number of iterations, and carefully setting the cross-selling conditions (to segment the customer portfolio and properly understand the combination of product–customer–occasion of use), we would gain a helpful insight into our customers' preferences and hence plan new product lines. Another benefit from this technique, besides an improved product portfolio, would be an increased reassurance that they will be accepted by our customer pool, allowing a significant cost reduction in terms of launching campaigns.

All in all, experience-based methodologies offer a significant improvement in terms of accurate, sincere responses, though they are obviously more expensive and require accurate planning.

3.2.2 Concentration Dimension

The Concentration dimension of value is the second stage of the TDV model. It aims to identify those agents and processes within a business value chain that account for the major part of added value out of the overall amount of it. That is to say, agents with an outstanding value proposition. We will refer to these agents and processes as the *value boosters* of the business. As we require a criteria to assess this added value, the analysis will be approached based on the conclusions of the Appreciation dimension (that is to say, according customer insights).

Applied Example: Fashion and Apparel

Imagine that we are considering the Concentration dimension for the fashion apparel and accessories business. Figure 3.5 depicts its simplified value chain, consisting of six different agents (and the customer).

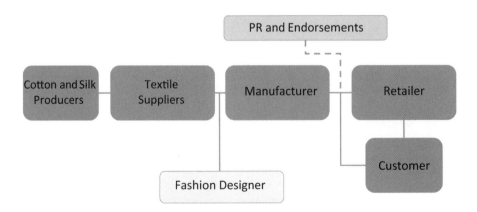

Figure 3.5   Apparel and accessories value chain (simplified)

Manufacturers, of course, are in the very center of the value chain. The Appreciation dimension analysis reveals some useful information:

1. The customer link type is relational, as the purchase of clothes has a strong aspirational background. Far from buying a mere piece of cloth, the process is much more related to an experience regarding status, self-esteem, beauty and success than to the product features themselves (although not totally, of course).

2. Considering this, and barring technical apparel for semi-pros (such as trekkers, skiers and similar), the mental links done by the customer in regards of said experience (how do I feel when I buy this product, who do I want to look like, what kind of message I want to launch to the world by wearing this product?) stands as significantly more important than any objective criteria (such as price, durability or even material).

3. Brand stands as a key attribute for the customer, thus explaining why two extraordinary similar pieces of cloth may significantly differ in terms of price as result of it (try comparing an H&M and a SuperDry hoodie if you don't believe me).

4. As with any other experience-based relationship (Figure 3.3), apparel purchasing is strongly related to an occasion of use, a type of mood and a certain degree of loyalty. In fact, it is commonly conceptualized as an activity (namely, shopping), and hence significantly influenced by the service and location layers. Buying a pullover or a skirt online is quite different to doing it in a physical store.

5. In a much sharper way than other consumer goods (such as, for example, yoghourts or a toner cartridge) purchasing clothes has an important social dimension. This causes the salience of a specific role: the prescriber. By prescriber we understand not only the person transmitting the brand values, but the adviser providing counseling (maybe the shopping companion or the shop assistant) and critical assessment (someone whom we seek approval from).

Given this information, we should be able to identify the value boosters of the business by linking the different value proposition with the customer insights. Note that a good way of approaching this is to translate the final economic value of the purchased good or service into diverse *shares of value* added by the different agents involved. You may want to think of it as a chain of individual margins (understood as the difference between incomes and outcomes) added by the different agents. We'll review this shortly.

In the case at hand, the gravity center of the business has clearly moved from its initial tangible-based positioning to an intangible one. Thus, what our grandmothers might have considered a good pair of trousers, for example, is likely to significantly differ from our perception nowadays. Now who are the current *value boosters* for this business? Well, those providing the valuable stages of the experience, according to the customer insights: the initial prescribers (PR and endorsement), the aspirational background creators (brands) and those related to the occasion of use and service layer (retailers). In fact, the economic translation of this value allocation (shares of value) pretty much coincides with this conclusion. Take a well-known fashion manufacturer, such as Gucci. Which part of its price is explained by the outstanding retail policy (shops located in the best streets of fashionable big cities), the celebrity endorsements (the pop singer Rihanna, for example) and, all in all, by the aspirational value of brands (luxury, status and so on)? And which part is explained by the extraordinary (so to speak) durability and resistance of its products or its exclusive textile fabric suppliers? Although some of these quality attributes may well apply (though not always), it is very obvious that these are not the main reasons for purchasing an item from Gucci.[3] What about value boosters for this business? Well, those agents operating within the initial stages of the value chain (such as textile fabrics suppliers or specialized machinery manufacturers) are not among them. This is precisely why brand is one of the biggest factors in capturing the biggest share of the economic return?: It's much more profitable to be present where the value is created (retail, brand).

Note how value boosters may differ greatly depending on the business, and also that a business is not defined and characterized just by the product (refer again to the example of technical clothing compared to fashion clothing: both drivers of competitiveness and customer insights are definitely different). This is why the stages of the TDV model demand a thorough and customized analysis: no competitive scenario can be simply inferred from a similar one, even if there's a strong resemblance between the purchased products in each one of them.

3.2.3 Predation Dimension

The Predation dimension of value is the third and last stage of the TDV model. It aims to identify those agents and processes within a business value chain that subtract value to the overall process or product/service, namely *value drainers*. This is a controversial statement, so let's try to clarify some licit doubts arising from it before attempting any methodological approach to the value drainers identification:

1. What do we mean, by subtracting value? Can the value in a business actually be subtracted?

Yes. Just as it is possible to identify processes and agents accounting for the most significant part of added value (and therefore, economic margin), it is also perfectly

---

3   We will review the Gucci-like model in depth in Chapter 4 and examine the Premium concept which encapsulates this thinking.

feasible to identify those not contributing to it. From this point of view, any process within a value chain that does not add value is subtracting it, just as waiting times do when you catch a flight (flight transportation business), traffic jams do while commuting (urban mobility business) or the need to be permanently reachable within an specific location to have a conversation before the advent of mobile phones did. Would we eliminate them from the equation, should it be possible? Most definitely. In fact, we've already done it in the case of the mobile phone!

2. Who determines whether an agent is eventually subtracting value?

The customer and, subsequently, market-based indicators (we'll see which ones shortly). The answer to this question lies at the very core of the TDV model, and as such it has been emphasized repeatedly: value is a customer-related concept, and therefore business agents are evaluated based on their contribution to the overall added value. On the other hand, market-based indicators are always a trustworthy way of identifying an increasing perception of little added value: unlike opinions or ideas, they are fact-based and aligned with the primary source of wealth: the customer.

3. How is the business dealing with said value drainers?

Most competitive scenarios basically don't allow those parts within a business value chain that are undesired or unrequired to be directly eliminated, either for technological reasons (as in the mobile phone example above), regulatory issues or simply a lack of sufficiently developed alternatives. However, it's just a matter of time. At this point, it's important to understand that value drainers will eventually be dismissed from competing, the only question is when. However, if not countered, value drainers will impact the overarching value proposition to the point of severely compromising the operating feasibility of those agents (even value boosters) which are exposed to them.

Now let's focus on how to possibly identify value drainers within a business. There are three potential sources of information, which should be combined to attain better results:

1. Customers' insights and behaviors regarding potential improvement on the whole business process and agent involvement

Remember the old statement about customer complaints being the most precious treasure for innovators? Well, it's basically true. As customers are typically more prone to complaints rather than compliments, it's reasonably easy to capture insights on areas for improvement and potential value drainers by both analyzing customer behavior and questioning them directly. The methodology described earlier and summarized in Figure 3.4 is perfectly valid and applicable, though some specific patterns might be helpful regarding how customer approach value drainers.

- *Always look at the entire value chain, not only at the well-known and obvious parts.* Customers assess the final product or service on an overall basis, and not as a combination of isolated parts. Imagine that you are going out for dinner with your partner, looking for a very special night out. What kind of place would you be looking for? Maybe an expensive restaurant, with high-quality food, superb atmosphere and great service. This is the obvious answer, but you might want to expand it. If you live in a suburban area and your desired restaurant is located in the city center, you are also concerned about issues such as parking facilities, traffic jams, sobriety checkpoints and, in case you've got kids, babysitter availability during weekends. Which of these criteria contribute to having a great night out? All of them. If one fails your night would be ruined from an overall perspective. As a restaurant owner, only some of them naturally lie within your powers (food, service and so on), but all of them affect your final success. Ignoring this fact is the fastest path to failure. Think twice: are you really unable to consider them? Because somebody will! For example Let Me Drive, a UK-based company, offers a driver service for those Londoners unable or unwilling to drive their own car to return home after a night out. The main difference from a taxi service is that they drive you home in your own car, and return back to headquarters by using a tiny folding motorbike previously stored in the car's luggage rack.
- *Value drainers are typically tolerated, rather than accepted.* This means attempting to substitute the agents that subtract value with a more suitable alternative. Not everybody is either interested or able to do so, but as the value subtraction grows bigger or the alternatives more available, more and more players try to adopt them. Think about how photo-developing shops, for example, have quickly declined in number. Home printers and cloud storage services have dramatically impacted on their business model, severely dependent on household customers. Early adopters started printing photos at home or simply storing them away on hard drives much before it become a global trend, just because it was cheaper, customized and self-controlled (apparently, not everybody likes a stranger to take a look at their personal photographs). A careful analysis would have foreseen a subsequent major change in the business before it took place.

2. Translate value offering into customer terms

For those agents or processes with an unclear translation, you have a candidate for a value drainer. By customer terms we mean a practical understanding of the value offering from the demand perspective. Most of the agents tend to directly associate value with its product or service (review Section 2.1 for a detailed explanation), while the customer-focused offerings are more much more revealing and useful.

Let's practice this concept: take the automotive business, for example, and try to conceptualize its value chain based on the customer perspective.

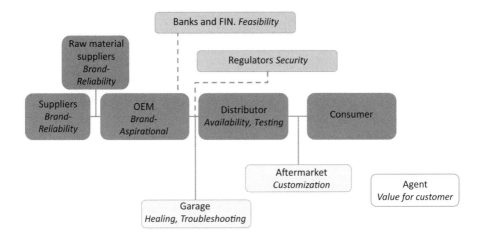

Figure 3.6   The automotive business value chain (simplified)

Applied Example: Automotive Business

Figure 3.6 offers a simplified version of the automotive value chain. For each agent, we have included a translation of its value offering into customer language (see the terms in italics). Let's review how different the final result might be depending on the perspective.

- Suppliers:
    - Offer-focused: Auto-parts, spare-parts.
    - Customer-focused: All kinds of tier-1 and tier-2 suppliers basically offer whatever reliability condition we mentally link to the brand as a whole (we choose a premium brand for different reasons,[4] quality normally being one of them).
- Original Equipment Manufacturers—OEM (carmakers):
    - Offer-focused: Car.
    - Customer-focused: Brand. All kinds of aspirational attributes of the brand are delivered by the brand itself (status, success and so on). This added value is easily acknowledged with a simple example: if you tried to sell a BMW or Porsche with no brand icons or symbols you would notice a dramatic decrease in its market price. Obviously, it would have nothing to do with the tangible features of the car so we should conclude that brand is monetizable.[5]

---

4   The premium concept is fully covered in section 4.4.7.
5   Chapter 4 covers the assessment of different business models which are leveraged on brand.

- Distributor:
  - Offer-focused: Car (life is simple when you think like a product).
  - Customer-focused: *Availability, testing.* Having a car dealer in your vicinity prevents you from having to travel to the car factory to buy your new car (or rather visit every single private individual seller for second-hand ones) as well as allowing a test drive before actually purchasing it. This is very important, as, for a wide array of consumers, testing is a vital precondition in many purchasing processes. In fact, and speaking generically, one of the main reasons why some users dismiss online purchasing, for example, is because of the inability to test the items beforehand.
- Banks and finance institutions:
  - Offer-focused: Loans.
  - Customer-focused: *Feasibility.* A huge percentage of buyers are simply unable to buy a car if it cannot be paid for in installments. From this perspective, the financial institutions simply make an otherwise impossible operation real. Thus, the love–hate relationship most customers have with their banks is easily understood: this strong dependence causes a powerful underlying emotional background.
- Garage:
  - Offer-focused: Repair service.
  - Customer-focused: *Healing, troubleshooting.* For most customers, a broken car is a major problem. Not only because of the strong dependence on it for their everyday life, but also due to the emotional link that many of them have with it. In other words: a steam iron is fixed, a car is healed. Even for those with a much colder approach, a garage is at least a place for trouble shooting, and hence the sky-high prices we tolerate: the value generated by an efficient troubleshooter is proportional to the anxiety provoked by the trouble itself.
- Regulators and insurance companies:
  - Offer-focused: Insurances.
  - Customer-focused: *Security.* Why do we tend to purchase comprehensive car insurances when renting a car abroad, especially if we are first-time visitors? The obvious answer is because we feel insecure in an unknown and potentially hazardous environment, and we are willing to pay whatever requested to be discharged from any liability. In other words: we exchange money for security. On another scale, the same thing happens at home. As in some past examples, this strong emotional scenario is severely conditioning all business processes (pricing, type of service, loyalty and so on).
- Aftermarket shops:
  - Offer-focused: Aftermarket products.
  - Customer-focused: *Customization.* All new cars are identical as they come out of the factory. The necessity of being different, special or distinguishable from the rest is a cross insight for many customers.

Aftermarket products and services provide the possibility to turn something generic, a commodity, into something customized that communicates a message to the rest of the world: its owner's message.

What do we get by approaching the value chain in this way? To begin with, a much broader perspective on potential competitors: instead of looking at the product or service, we analyze what our customer takes from it, hence enabling once-hidden competitors (we should consider our competitor to be whoever is trying to pose a solution for the same customer need as ours, and not just the one offering the same product). Secondly, this approach will eventually uncover the hidden value drainers of the business chain: all agents with an unclear, confused or too complicated customer-focused value proposition are definitely strong candidates.

3. Analyze resource consumption within the value chain and link it with customer insights

While the first and second approaches are of a qualitative nature, this one is essentially quantitative and raises a framework for analysis based on the assessment of resource consumption. To make it simple: processes and agents consuming a high volume of available resources within a value chain are potential candidates for value drainers. What kind of resources are we referring to? The very same ones a factory manager would use to assess the efficiency of a production system: *time* and *money*. A specific step within a production system that significantly increases the overall processing time might be a bottleneck and hence negatively affect the global process (a particular employee or manager can also be a bottleneck, and sometimes this is pretty obvious just by looking at the company's organizational chart), unless there are solid reasons to justify it (for example, a mandatory quality inspection or a complex mechanization process). And even in this case, they are permanently tracked in pursuit of optimization, just to make sure that there are really no better choices or improvements. So, moving back to business analysis ... are all processes with high resource consumption value drainers? Not at all, just those with little, decreasing or no value for the customer (note how customer insights always stand as the ultimate benchmark). Why? Because *slow* and *expensive* are, on first impression, negative qualities. We may come to accept these processes in exchange for a valuable outcome, but in most cases we are just tolerating them. Remember what we mentioned earlier when speaking of the general concept of value: a process or an agent within a value chain can only be mentally tagged as valuable or not valuable. For those tagged as 'not valuable', the only possible conditions are for them to be dismissed or *not yet* dismissed. Let's look for expensive and slow processes, then!

Up to this point, we have been reviewing how to identify value drainers based on different cues and information sources. Now that we know what they are, let's concentrate on what they do: predate value or, from another perspective, predate margin.

Margin predation

Michael Porter initially introduced the analysis of the impact of both suppliers and customers as competitive forces in his 1979 article "How Competitive Forces Shape Strategy." These concepts were further included in his popular model of Five Forces to analyze business competitiveness, turning into a broadly used pattern for analysis that is still in use. In line with our overarching thread, we will be approaching them from a value-focused perspective.

As already explained, a value booster accounts for a significant amount of delivered value within a business. We also know that this value can be translated into economic value (monetized). From the customer perspective, this reflected value is directly linked to the price paid (the money the customer has to pay in exchange for the value), whereas from the agent perspective, it is linked with the cost (the cost I have to assume to deliver this value, namely the margin). This means that every process in which an agent is involved can be analyzed from a trade-off perspective, based on the general value criteria determined by the customer insights. Some processes within a value chain, however, are not visible enough for the final customer, at least in terms of money and time. They do affect him, as they impact some tangible attributes (final good price or overall processing time required), but are simply unknown so cannot be directly assessed by the process explained in Figure 3.3. To properly analyze them, we require an individual analysis for every value booster of the business (as they account for the biggest share of value) and its downstream and upstream relationships within the value chain.

For every value booster, we shall consider the difference between the delivered value (and, consequently, the economic income) and the supported costs to deliver its *margin*. Every value booster (in fact, every business agent) is permanently in contact with both upstream and downstream agents (those located directly before and after the value booster within the value chain). We shall generically refer to the upstream agents as *suppliers*. A supplier will be anybody delivering any product or service required by the value booster (typically, spare parts and raw materials, but also know-how, man-hours or any professional service). In this simplified scheme, even employees are supplier, as they supply the value booster with their work. On the other hand, we shall refer to the downstream agents as *customers*. A customer will be anybody buying from the value booster, and therefore includes both final customers and distributors (a generic distributor is nothing but a trade customer). As Figure 3.7 depicts, the overall margin for a value booster can be conceptualized as the length of a spring. For any given value proposition, the maximum length of the spring (margin) is limited (above this limit, the spring would be broken).

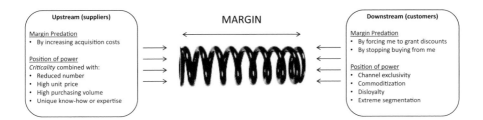

Figure 3.7   Margin Predation for value boosters

Below this limit, the spring is permanently pushed by both suppliers and customers. These opposed forces compress the spring, reducing its length and hence, consuming the free available margin. In other words, they predate the remaining margin for value boosters. If this is reduced, so is the delivered value for the final customer, hence resulting in an overall value Predation. This doesn't mean that suppliers and customers are evil and unnecessary to the core, just that in some specific situations they might act as value drainers.

Be that as it may, the force applied by suppliers and customers (the extent to which they are able to predate margin) is determined by their position of power compared to the value booster. The more powerful a supplier or a customer is, the higher the force applied and hence the margin predated. As summarized in Figure 3.7, this position of power is determined by a set of criteria. Suppliers consume margin by increasing acquisition costs. Dell, the computer manufacturer, needs to pay a specific amount of money to AMD, Intel or any other similar microprocessor manufacturers to install one of their products in its computers. If they increase the acquisition costs (in whatever way), Dell loses part of its margin. As simple as that. But... what if every other supplier did that? Could, for example, a keyboard manufacturer demand a similar increase for its product? It's not likely, due to its almost non-existing position of power. What enables the capacity to increase the acquisition costs for a given supplier? The answer is its criticality to the value booster, combined with some other criteria such as uniqueness, high unitary price or purchasing volume or a very specific know-how. Intel and AMD, for example, are critical to DELL because microprocessors are critical to a computer. Besides, how many competitive microprocessor manufacturers can be found in the market, compared to, for example, keyboard manufacturers? Obviously, fewer. Add to this the high unitary price and the challenging operating conditions (which require a very specific and advanced know-how) and you will understand how powerful they are compared to Dell itself, and therefore to what extent they can predate its margin. The same happens with football players and football clubs (football player salaries account for between 50 percent and 70 percent of total club incomes— try to do the math for any other type of industry and you will get the point).

Some might argue that this capacity to predate margin is directly proportional to the value generated, and hence nothing to be eliminated but fostered (just like any other value booster). While this is valid reasoning, it is essential to think in customer terms again. In the case of football clubs, without questioning the key importance of football players in the business, they are the ones making the business possible and delivering the basic product consumed (football matches). If the football players kept on predating their margin to the point where the clubs were simply forced into bankruptcy, who would play the football matches? Players alone can't, no matter how good they are. Besides, if the clubs were ruined, they would no longer be able to hire players and hence deliver value. It's important to note that football players are not value drainers just by themselves. They become value drainers as a result of their extraordinary impact on a club's accounting and value offering, caused by the reasons mentioned above.

As for the customers (including both final and trade ones), they predate the value margin by decreasing its incomes. There are two possible ways in which they can do this: by demanding discounts from it in order to continue purchasing or simply by stopping purchasing the product or service. Indeed, a discount may be a necessary evil, but an evil after all. Every single seller would choose not to have them, should it be possible. Of course, theory says that, when used within a limited time frame and combined with specific situations, such as a new product launching or to foster cross-selling, discounts prove useful. The problem arises when discounts become indispensable and sustained over time to retain the customer. Mobile operators, for example, constantly use discounts on handsets and monthly bills in order to prevent customers from running away. In fact, they even impose minimum term contracts on them. These types of clauses, unthinkable in businesses like consumer goods (would you imagine guaranteeing that you won't buy another brand of wine for whole year?), are a byword in many others. The customers' position of power increases either when there's a rising tendency toward commoditization on the supply side (all purchasing options are equally perceived by the consumer) that leads to a blatant customer disloyalty. However, provided that we're considering the case of value boosters (and, therefore, facing solid and appreciated value propositions), it is much more frequent to be facing a situation in which the position of power is the result of channel exclusivity or dominance in which the trade customer rules the distribution with iron fist, deciding which products, at what price and how many are sold. This is a very typical situation in a mass consumption business like consumer goods, in which huge distributors like WalMart (USA) or Mercadona (Spain) wield this kind of power. Again, we should refer to the conclusions of the Appreciation and Concentration of value stages to clearly identify the proper balance between shares of value of the different agents. In the abovementioned example, despite the sure value being added by the distributor in the consumer goods business, and despite the increasing salience of distributor brands, which are changing the traditional value perception (we'll be reviewing this point a bit further), the consumer is still choosing the product over the channel (at least, products with an appreciated value proposition). Would you rather buy a generic brand of cola sold in your everyday supermarket, or walk to the other side of the block to get your beloved Coke? So, who is really adding the value here? This situation works the other way around for other type of products, most typically those involved in a merely transactional purchase (remember the aluminum foil example explained in the Appreciation stage), in which the distributor may turn into a value booster itself. Again, it is very important to accurately follow the steps of the TDV model to obtain a useful sequence of results.

To conclude this example… what would happen if the channel dominance was so strong that it could simply eliminate all Coke from every single supermarket for many kilometers around? Would you still drive (or walk) the distance to get it? Maybe yes, but just because it's Coke! Many (the immense majority) of products included in our shopping list, however, would simply be replaced by the available choices given by the distributor. This channel dominance would strongly impact the value booster (private labels, in this example) margin, subsequently its R+D and marketing investment and therefore the value delivered to the final customer.

The last way in which customers can represent a Predation of Value is extreme segmentation. By segmentation we understand variations of different products and services to different groups of your customer base in order to increase market share and improve revenues. The final goal would be to improve the customer adaptation of the product portfolio. However, it's very important to understand that segmentation is always a defensive strategy. Let's explain it: as the competition level within a business grows, the customer starts gaining power. If no disruptive value proposition arises (review the blue ocean example explained in Section 2.1), and competitors basically compete on already existing ones, customers essentially demand a permanently increasing degree of product customization in order to keep purchasing it. Customization may come in diverse forms, typically different physical, technological or pricing features. In order to maintain a threatened market share, and pushed by other competitors' similar strategies, a company might be compelled to start a segmentation race involving customer and product portfolio. The problem with segmentation is that it is expensive, both in terms of operating expenses (manufacturing and marketing more product references increases costs) and revenues (reducing the potential customer basis also reduces overall incomes). Note that it might be *necessary*, but not *chosen*. Companies attempt segmentation, therefore, as a defensive strategy. All of them would choose to have a unique, successful product for an almost unsegmented market! It may sound like a fairy tale, but we have a blatant reality of this situation: Apple's iPhone. Let's use a comparison between Apple and Nokia's evolution to close this section and practice what we have learned.

Applied Example: Apple versus Nokia

In 2007, the Finnish mobile phone manufacturer Nokia reached the peak of its success to date. The company sold 435 million mobile devices worldwide, accounting for almost 40,000 million euros. That year, Nokia reached the outstanding figure of 39 new handsets launched, at an average selling price (ASP) of 86€.

In June of that same year, the thus far computer manufacturer, Apple, launched a new and revolutionary product that was set to make history and change all competition rules: the iPhone. As with all disruptive innovations, the iPhone didn't simply offer significant improvements over the existing benchmarks, but represented the birth of a brand new category for the business (smartphones) which dramatically impacted the way people understood mobile communication and its interaction with the computer business. The competitors' adaptation to this major inrush was very diverse. Whereas some of them, like Samsung, successfully deployed a copycat strategy that would lead it towards market leadership (2013 figures), others blatantly failed to adapt to a new competition era, built upon completely different customer insights and therefore quickly faced problems. Nokia, needless to say, was one of them. Unable to understand the new diversity of competitiveness for its long-known business, which was largely migrating from a product-based to a service-based competition model, Nokia committed manifest mistakes regarding the selection of the operating system to run on its smartphones and the subsequent choice of a strategic partner. Though Microsoft's takeover of Nokia in 2014 has granted the Finnish company a second chance (Nokia may not yet have spoken its last word on the smartphone business), up to this point the comparison between its strategy and Apple's allows for an applied perspective of the Predation dimension of Value (Charts 3.2 to 3.8) embedded in a global review based on the TDV model approach. Let's review it:

Appreciation of Value: From a product-based business to a content-based one

- A first approach to the assessment of competitive issues for a company is based on the identification of the root cause of its problems. To put it simply, the origin of the trouble might be either found in the demand (or lack of demand, to be more specific) side, the supply side (an ill-defined business model, which automatically leads to an unsustainable cost structure) or a combination of both, this last situation typically being a last stage of one of the formers. Under the TDV model perspective, demand issues correspond to the Appreciation (identifying customer insights, hence value) and Concentration (creating and delivering a value proposition) analyses, whereas supply ones are mainly linked to the Predation analysis (carelessness or inability to solve an imbalance of the business model). Applying supply-focused solutions to demand problems, or vice versa, is therefore not likely to solve a crisis. However, though this might look pretty simple and obvious, experience shows that companies' responses to a crisis are much more frequently conditioned by short-term urgencies rather than coherent analysis. In the case of Nokia, its sales steadily declined from 2007 to 2012, showing a major disalignment with customer's insights (sales evolution is an ultimate metric for the Appreciation dimension of value.[6] Said insights indicated a clear evolution of the business concept and expected value that run parallel to the progressive deployment of the then-untapped potential of the Internet. As the business moved from a technology-based to a content-based focus, the customer link changed as well, from a customer acquisition emphasis (transactional link) to a customer retention one (relational link). The development of an experience and the progressive integration and deployment of content-adapted infrastructures and products, as a major expenditure and a new competitive requirement, must be passed on to the customer (at least partially). A good proof of Nokia's inability to do so is the sustained decline in its average handset selling price (Chart 3.7), compared to Apple's. Indeed, Nokia hesitated to abandon its traditional value proposition and target market while trying to understand the new competitive paradigm. It will soon become the deposed king: still reigning, yet in a dying business. Apple, instead, understood that, beyond the product approach, its core value proposition as a computer manufacturer and software developer was essentially coincident with the new customer insights

- It is important to note that, as explained in point 1 of the value drainers' identification process, the room for improvement (in terms of delivered value) may not lie just within the traditional places (in the case of mobile phones, product physical features), but any other stage of the value chain. This, needless to say, is especially important when facing major competitive changes caused by disruptive innovations such as those mentioned above. In the case of mobile devices, the new workhorse after the rise of the iPhone was software development and its capacity to provide product customization. Nokia simply ignored this, whereas Apple delivered superior customer experience leveraged on its outstanding product features and software-based services like the App Store in a moment in which all its other competitors were simply unable to do it. The result was a devastating average revenue growth per year of 718 percent during the period 2008–10 and a more moderate, yet still awesome, 72 percent for 2011–13. Nokia sales, meanwhile, declined by 61 percent during the period 2007–12. In 2011, Apple outsold Nokia for the first time.

---

6   Chapter 5 offers a detailed explanation of the metric definition process and its link with the Appreciation dimension of value.

Concentration of Value: a transformed value chain with new dominant
contenders

- In line with the new value paradigm and its transition from voice phone to smartphone, new value boosters were aroused in the business. Compared to the traditional one (Figure 3.8), the resultant value chain (Figure 3.9) was much more complex, as it encompassed different types of non-native contenders and competitive drivers. The thus far vertically integrated manufacturers, such as Nokia, Motorola or Ericsson, were confronted by two main types of new competitors:
    - Non-native, highly specialized Internet products and services, leveraged on a software development or content generation expertise (such as, for example, Google, and, later on, Facebook). Their customer-focused share of value would be based on the product and service integration and customization, and hence were strongly linked to the customer experience (a key insight).
    - Non-native, consolidated companies from the personal computer, consumer electronics or hardware manufacturing businesses, with outstanding manufacturing capabilities better aligned with a new generation of product requirements (such as Apple, Microsoft and later on Samsung or Asus).

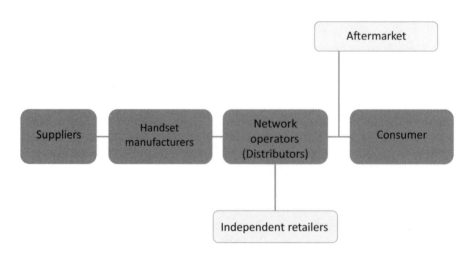

Figure 3.8   The traditional value chain of the mobile phone business

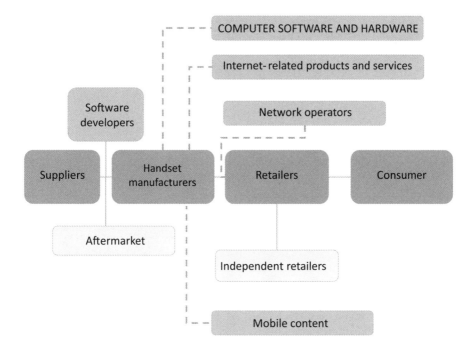

Figure 3.9   The new value chain for the smartphone business

- Nokia, until that point, had internalized all manufacturing and development activities (such as software development). The distribution of its products had been assumed mainly by network operators and a few independent retailers. Compared to that, and again in line with the new value paradigm that reinforced the customer experience (hence including shopping) and increased perceived value, the retail activities progressively gained importance within the new value chain. Apple, aware of this new aspirational background, invested in an aggressive retail policy that completely changed competition and Customer Relationship Management, while paying special attention to aftermarket revenues. Nokia, once again, was out of the game in that regard.

Predation of Value: Competing on old parameters

- Once the new competition rules for a given business are established, typically due to the rise of a new dominant contender (or a group of them), the role of all traditional agents, internal processes and tactics are inevitably reviewed. From that point of view, and as mentioned in Section 3.2, what doesn't add value is actually subtracting it. In the Nokia case, the company tried to fight back by using its traditional tactics and weapons, which ultimately led to a severe margin Predation (Chart 3.4) caused by the new role as value drainers coming from the supplier and customer requirements: operating expenses and extreme segmentation. Basically, Nokia was trying to compete by continuously launching new products, while the new competition rules had drifted toward a strategic management of key assets (technologic design, but primarily brand). Take a look at some of the evidence:

- Apple launched one new iPhone model per year during the period 2007–12 (from the original iPhone to iPhone 5, launched in September, 2012), and two new models in 2013 (iPhone 5S and 5C). Whereas the original iPhone and iPhone 3G (2008) were just offered in black color, Apple introduced white covers in 2009 and kept it like that until 2013, when its iPhone 5C and 5S models were sold in five and three different colors respectively. Besides the choice of internal memory size for their iPhones, the company progressively moved (Chart 3.2) from an almost completely unsegmented initial value proposition in 2007, with two different iPhone models manufactured, to a segmented strategy in 2013, with 29 iPhone models manufactured. As shown in Chart 3.2, there is a positive correlation between the available references per year and the total number of handsets sold, thus showing a proper deployment of the segmentation strategy that complies with its original purpose: a better adaptation to the customer basis.

  – While Apple launched said eight different models from 2007 to 2013, Nokia launched 226 (the total number of manufactured handsets per year, considering colors and other features is simply countless). Anyway, Apple was born a niche player, whereas Nokia had always played the market leader role and hence targeted a broader customer basis, so this information is not concluding by itself. However, as depicted in Chart 3.5, the total number of handsets sold per year during the period 2007–12 fell fairly steadily. Segmentation, as we have already explained, is expensive and, for Nokia, seemingly useless. Probably aware of this situation, the company significantly reduced the number of annual launches, moving from an average of 42 during 2007–9 to 25 during 2010–12. However, this proved useless: Nokia was already a victim of extreme segmentation, surely in a desperate attempt to regain customer acceptance but still without paying attention to the real value disalignment. As shown in Chart 3.8, Apple needed increasingly less marketing expenditure to sell one handset, compared to Nokia. This difference peaked in 2012, when Apple needed to spend 60 percent less in market expenditure than Nokia to sell a mobile phone. It's worth highlighting, as a curiosity, that, as stated by Apple's top management during the trial against Samsung in 2012, Apple invested no money in advertising the original iPhone in 2007 (Fiegerman, 2012): so disruptive was the new value proposition that the mass media did it for them.

  – Extreme segmentation, conditioned by a lack of effective weapons to confront the increasing power of the customer, and combined with fewer handsets sold, resulted in higher overheads per unit sold.

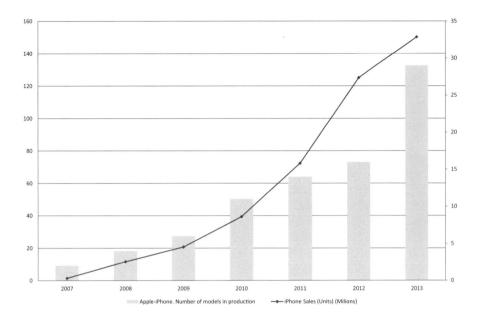

Apple-iPhone. Number of models in production   —◆—iPhone Sales (Units) (Milions)

Chart 3.2   Apple's figures I
Source: Data from Apple Press Info 2007–14; Apple Group Financial Reports 2011–14; List of iOs Devices, n.d.

> Besides, Nokia was absolutely unable to pass these costs on to its customers: as shown in Chart 3.7, the ASP (a very common metric in the business) per handset not only did not rise, but dropped from 86€ in 2007 to 47€ in 2012. During the very same period, Apple's ASP (unsubsidized) constantly grew, peaking in 2011 with almost 500€. Not only was Apple able to sell more iPhones, but at a higher price and through an accurate and thorough segmentation strategy, therefore totally avoiding customers' margin Predation.
>
> – Regarding suppliers' margin Predation, as shown in Chart 3.3, Apple basically obliterated it during the period 2007–13. The manufacturing costs (acquisition costs, as explained in the model) for the consecutive models launched after the original iPhone were always kept under 200$, despite the increasing ASP. The gross margin, therefore, rose in an almost sustained way during the period, and therefore increased Apple's capacity to deliver further value as a major value booster.

All in all, this competitive scenario is a good example of severe value Predation and poor analysis of customer insights, resulting in a very complicated situation for Nokia. Speaking in terms of resource consumption, we may conclude that the combination of margin Predation forced by customers (extreme segmentation, rising marketing costs, lowering average selling prices) and suppliers (manufacturing costs) caused a major decrease in profitability.

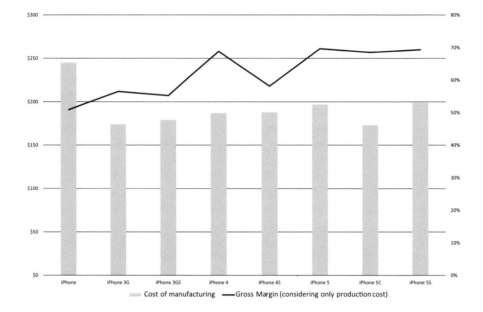

Chart 3.3   Apple's figures II
Source: Data from IHS Technology 2009 and 2013; Statista 2012.

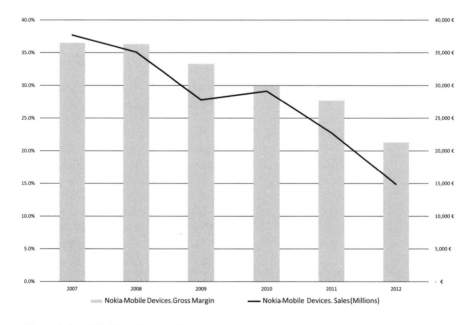

Chart 3.4   Nokia's figures I
Source: Data from Nokia Group Annual Reports 2007–12.

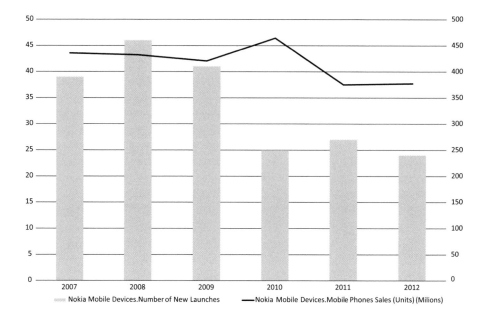

Chart 3.5   Nokia's figures II

Source: Data from Nokia Group Annual Reports 2007–212; Inofon 2013.

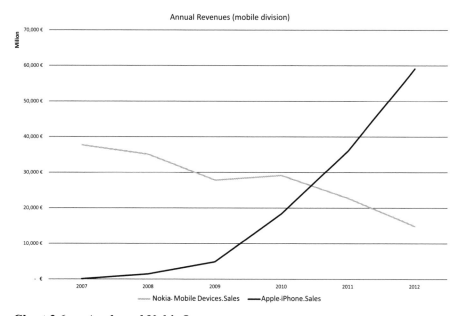

Chart 3.6   Apple and Nokia I

Source: Data from Nokia Group Annual Reports 2007–12; Apple Press Info 2007–14;
Apple Group Financial Reports 2011–14.

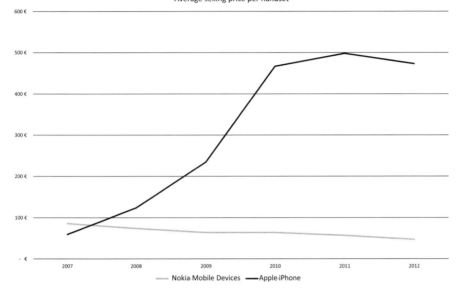

Chart 3.7 Apple and Nokia II
Source: Data from Nokia Group Annual Reports 2007–12; Apple Press Info 2007–14; Apple Group Financial Reports 2011–14.

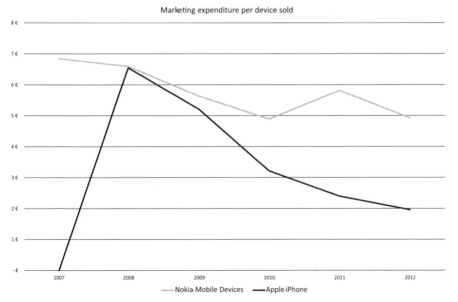

Chart 3.8 Apple and Nokia III
Source: Data from Nokia Group Annual Reports 2007–12; Apple Press Info 2007–14; Apple Group Financial Reports 2011–14; Dediu 2013.

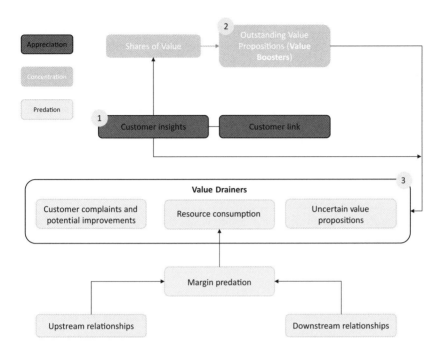

Figure 3.10   The TDV model: conceptual mapping

3.3 THE TDV MODEL: KEY TAKEAWAYS AND CONCEPTUAL MAPPING

- The TDV model defines a comprehensive methodology to analyze the drivers of competitiveness within a business. As such, it stands as the keystone of the external analysis, defining a step-by-step guideline that has the business value flow as its leitmotif (Figure 3.10).
- The analysis poses an analytical process divided into three different stages, covering the respective dimensions of value within a business: *Appreciation, Concentration and Predation*.
- The Appreciation dimension of value aims is the first one to be assessed. Its essential goals are twofold. On the one hand, it aims to identify the customer expectations and insights regarding what is valuable, and therefore, appreciated and required. On the other hand, it also determines the dominant type of relationship between the customer and the business agents (*customer link*).
- There are two basic procedures to capture customer insights: asking and experiencing. Both are to be combined, though the second one significantly enriches the final result by revealing sincere and real-life-based information.
- There are two possible types of customer links: transactional (essentially price-based) and relational (involving a sustained relationship through the

creation of experiences). Although both of them might result in successful strategies, the relational link poses a competitive advantage for the company, as a result of the fostering of customer loyalty.

- The Concentration dimension of value is the second stage of the TDV model. It aims to identify those agents and processes within a business value chain that account for the major part of added value, and therefore offer an outstanding value proposition. These agents are called *value boosters*.
- Value boosters can be identified by comparing the different value propositions with the customer insights. A good way of doing it is translating the final economic value of the purchased good or service into diverse *shares of value* added by the different agents involved. Value boosters account for outstanding shares of value.
- The Predation dimension of value is the third and last stage of the TDV model. It aims to identify those agents and processes within a business value chain that subtract value. They are called *value drainers*.
- Customer insights and subsequent market-based indicators determine if an agent or process is subtracting value.
- In the long run, value drainers are always dismissed from competition. However, if exposed long enough to them, other agents might see its operating feasibility compromised (even value boosters).
- There are three complimentary approaches to value drainer identification: *customer complaints and potential improvements*, *unclear value propositions* and *excessive resource consumption.*
- Customer complaints show progressive disalignments with new dominant value paradigms or unsatisfactory processes. This might be originated anywhere within the entire value chain.
- Unclear value propositions arise from the translation of value offerings into customer terms (instead of product/service terms). Those of them confused or too complicated are strong candidates for a value drainer.
- Agents or processes consuming excessive resources might be value drainers. Essential resources are *time* and *money.*
- The difference between the value delivered by a business agent and the amount of resources (costs) required to deliver it is called its margin. Margin can be predated by both upstream and downstream relationships within a value chain.
- Upstream relationships of a business agents are called its suppliers. Downstream ones, its customers.
- *Margin Predation* from suppliers is forced by increasing costs.
- *Margin Predation* from customers is forced by either compelling discounts or the quitting of buying.
- In order for customers and suppliers to be able to predate margin, they require a position of power. This position of power is determined by specific competitive scenarios. If not minimized, these types of situations will threaten the capacity to deliver the value of the business agent, and therefore impact the whole business and the final customer.

CHAPTER 4

THE INTERNAL CREATION OF VALUE

4.1 APPROACH

Planning and deploying a winning business strategy is pretty much like playing chess. The only difference is that quite frequently you don't get the chance to start a fresh game, but simply join it in mid-play and try to do your best, given your situation. Some players believe that they can win the game by simply starting playing and relying on a lucky strike, their self-confidence or just by inertia. Although this might actually happen from time to time, such players will obviously lose an overwhelming number of games. To maximize the chances of success, thorough players would first of all start gathering information about chess rules and allowed movement of the pieces. Right after the general competition rules are understood, they should pay attention to the current state of the game: who's leading and how their opponents are leveraging the available resources to do so. Drawing a parallel with the guidelines of strategic analysis, this is what the external analysis aims for. Once done, it's time for the players to start looking at their own weapons: what do they have left and how can they use it to win the game, given the current situation? Internal analysis is aiming for these answers, which by the way are rarely unique: just like a chess games, the paths leading to victory are multiple and depend both on the player and the opponent. However, although the selected strategy might be different in every situation, the basic steps leading to it, both in a chess game and in a business strategy, always remain the same. Before we move on to their definition, we need to emphasize some of the traits of a winning value proposition.

As we have already noted, the ultimate objective for every company is to maximize the value delivered to its customers. *Maximize* is a relative term, and therefore we are implying that a company value proposition will be constantly confronted and compared with those of its competitors. This involves that, in order to hold a chance, a value proposition needs to be *easily identifiable* on one hand, and *better*, on the other. The former is due to the need to stand out in a crowded competitive scenario, in which customers have a limited attention span. Regarding the latter, we will be discussing throughout this chapter the ways in which we can be *better* than our competitors, but so far it's essential to understand that, when it comes to competition, *better* means, above all, *different*.

Hence, the internal analysis will be dealing with the creation of value within the company boundaries, regarding the drivers of competitiveness spotted during the external analysis through the TDV model. Every company can enable and boost this value through what we shall call *internal levers for value generation*. We will learn how to dimension and use them in order to achieve the *corporate goals*, the very first step in the definition of our strategy, and be positioned in the market according to a clearly identifiable *competitive model*. It's time to move our pieces and start playing the game!

4.1.1 The Internal Analysis Guidelines

Figure 4.1 gathers the different steps within the internal analysis, as well as the conceptual tools that we will be using for each one of them. The process is based on three major steps that lead to the delivery of value to the business in general and the customer in particular.

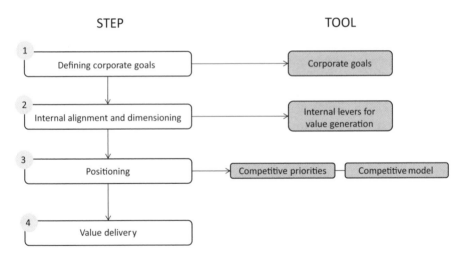

Figure 4.1   The internal analysis guidelines

1. *Defining the corporate goals*: As we mentioned in the chess example, whereas the overall objective is to maximize the delivered value, this can be achieved in different ways: you can be adding an equivalent amount of value by eliminating an unprofitable process, enhancing customer experience or improving your overall value proposition (or a combination of them). As we will see, each one of these ways is linked

to a stage of the TDV model (to ensure model coherence and integrity). This said, it is important to understand that the usefulness of the corporate goal definition lies in its capacity to translate the global strategic approach to competition into operating, tangible terms (and, therefore, enable a further consolidation of the competitive model and corporate identity). In other words, concerning the definition of corporate goals, the gains from the analytic procedure in itself, together with the subsequent process monitoring that entails, are much more important than the exact accuracy of the goals or even their level of achievement, for some of these are to be revised and adjusted according to changes in the competitive scenario and corporate performance. From this point of view, a useful goal is the one that gathers the entire company (within its different layers) around a common idea of competition, enables a learning process, promotes accountability and fosters employee empowerment.

2. *Aligning all your internal resources to serve the global strategy and goals.* In line with point 1, this represents the very core of the internal analysis and is the most determinant factor of corporate success. Indeed, once the goals are clearly set, all available resources in the company must be aligned with its pursuit. In plain words, if your primary objective is to reduce operating costs by 15 percent, every single process, employee and division needs to be committed to it in the same proportion. To influence this value generation, a company may have at its disposal a set of internal levers. By dimensioning and deploying these internal levers according to the desired goals, the value is generated and further delivered to the business and customer.

3. *Defining a clear competitive model and positioning it in the business.* Based on the match between the identified drivers of competitiveness, the corporate goals and the core assets and capabilities, a company must define a competitive model by which it can be clearly identified and valued in the market. The competitive model is created by a combination of different competitive priorities (defined as *a specific focus and approach toward competition leveraged on a differential corporate competence*) that has an entity in itself. The concept of competitive model is absolutely essential, as it's a way to link the corporate brand (its most valuable market asset, as we will see in Chapter 5) to a set of attributes, values and promises that constitutes the core of the value proposition and also provides an internal benchmark that defines the guidelines for every corporate decision and aligns all internal resources toward a common goal.

4. *Value delivery.* A company with a clear understanding of the drivers of competitiveness and the value framework within a business, based upon which it has defined a solid, identifiable competitive model levered by its internal capabilities and core assets, is now able to deliver value accordingly. The corporate brand stands as the primary market asset for the company, representing both its most powerful communication tool and a key to appreciate the business reaction to its value proposition.

4.2 DEFINING THE CORPORATE GOALS

In Lewis Carroll's celebrated *Alice's Adventures in Wonderland* (1865), Alice Liddell, the main character, and the Cheshire Cat, a recurrent enigmatic character, hold this conversation:

> *Alice: Would you tell me, please, which way I ought to go from here?*
> *The Cheshire cat: That depends a good deal on where you want to get to.*
> *Alice: I don't much care where.*
> *The Cheshire Cat: Then it doesn't much matter which way you go.*
> *Alice: So long as I get somewhere.*
> *The Cheshire cat: Oh, you're sure to do that, if only you walk long enough.*

It is no secret that Lewis Carroll's work is a well-known source for management tips, probably due to the fact that the frequently ambiguous meaning of the dialogues leaves much for subjective interpretation and, therefore, is applicable to a wide range of disciplines, but also because of the bewildering reasoning of most of its characters, who systematically question the most commonly accepted rules of behavior, compelling Alice (and the reader) to review the basis of the conventional wisdom from a critical point of view. In the dialogue above, the Cheshire Cat makes a critical point about a frequent characteristic of today's competition: the primacy of action over reflection. Indeed, being time-related parameters (such as time-to-market or lead time), as crucial as they are in such a harsh competitive environment, the emphasis is increasingly set on the handling of time as the unique truly relevant factor. Thus, we are witnessing the emergence of time-framed strategic analysis, competitive advantages, profit structures and business models (the Hypercompetition[1] model might be a good example). A misapplication (or an overemphasis) of these principles, however, might lead to inefficient managerial procedures: as stated before, the process of defining corporate goals has an importance in itself, firstly because it forces a review of all internal processes under an accountable perspective, and secondly because it helps the staff to gain focus on the expected outcomes and enhances visibility on the corporate strategy. This approach to the definition of objectives as a tool for employee empowerment and corporate realignment is absolutely key, and as such will be further reviewed throughout the chapter (especially while assessing the corporate levers for the internal creation of value in Section 4.3)

This said, and turning now to some key points about corporate goals and how they fit into our value-based main thread, the takeaway message from the Cheshire Cat's statements is twofold:

---

1   D'Aveni, 1994.

1. There is no strategy without objectives. From this point of view, corporate goals are the primary benchmark against which to assess the obtained results and the feasibility of the planned strategy.
2. Corporate goals are neither good nor bad, appropriate nor inappropriate in themselves (at most, they might be wrongly or inaccurately defined). Almost everything might look reasonable enough, so that you better make sure that you establish them according to valid criteria. As the Cheshire Cat says, you will eventually get somewhere if you start walking: make sure your final destination is worth the walk.

Precisely for this reason, to ensure the coherence and validity of corporate goals, we will set the objectives according to the same structure and obtained conclusions of the external analysis. Following the very same structure of the TDV model, we shall define three different types of objectives, each one of them focused on a specific dimension of value generation (Figure 4.2). To do so, we'll think of our company as if it was a restaurant and classify our objectives according to its different areas and roles. In this sense, a simplified representation of a restaurant allows us to identify three different roles within the staff that enables an intuitive classification: those attending the customers (we'll generically call them *waiters*), those preparing the meals (*cooks*) and those working in the back office (*sweepers*). Each one of these roles is equally important to ensure a feasible operating model and a powerful value proposition, just as the TDV model describes a proper approach to value drivers based on different dimensions. Hence, each one of them has specific areas of competence and related objectives.

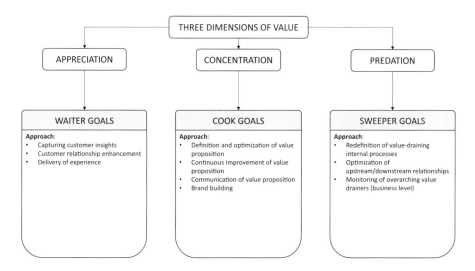

Figure 4.2   The definition of corporate goals

1. The *waiter* is responsible for serving and attending the customers, and hence is the person in the restaurant that best knows what they want and how they want it. In a direct equivalence with the TDV Model, the waiter is the main person responsible for the *Appreciation* dimension of value. Therefore, among the corporate goals, the waiter ones are those related to the processes of capturing customer insights, enhancing customer relationships and improving the delivery of experience. Examples for waiter goals could be defining the specific retail policy, dimensioning a Customer Relationship Management system, gathering customer information and data or dimensioning and deploying a commercial policy.

2. The *cook* is responsible for preparing the meals, and hence the core asset of the value proposition. Speaking in terms of the TDV model, the cook is responsible for the *Concentration* dimension of value. Therefore, all corporate goals aiming to define, improve or optimize the value proposition, as well as communicate it and build the corporate brand as the main market asset, fall into this category. Examples of cook goals could be all kinds of branding activity, the planning of corporate strategy or the accurate definition of product and service portfolio (both in manufacturing and operating terms).

3. The *sweeper* is responsible for cleaning and keeping the overall activity as tidy and focused as possible. This approach of *waste processing* matches with the *Predation* stage of the TDV model, since they both focus on the control and elimination of every process that may be draining value from the global proposition. Hence, the sweeper goals are those linked with the redefinition of value-draining internal processes, the optimization of upstream and downstream relationships which are potentially hazardous and the constant monitoring of business-level value drainers. Examples of sweeper goals might be the definition of internal KPIs, the implementation of a balanced scorecard (or whatever type of quality control process), the redefinition of supplier policies or the creation of a technological surveillance service.

Apart from embedding every corporate goal in this general structure, it is essential to ensure their proper and accurate definition. As we mentioned before, strategies may be adequate or inadequate, and corporate goals properly or wrongly defined. Pursuing an inaccurate or ludicrous goal linked to a visionary and disruptive strategy will prove just as dangerous and time-wasting as choosing a bad strategy. So, what kind of requirements must a corporate goal meet? Doran (1981) conceptualized the answer to this question proposing a useful mnemonic acronym. A good objective is a SMART objective.

- S stands for *Specific*, meaning that the definition of the goal must leave no room for ambiguities or confronted interpretations. For example, instead of saying "improve quality standards," we may say "improve customer complaints regarding the laptop repair service."

- M stands for *Measurable*, meaning that it must add significant quantitative and qualitative information to ensure its traceability and monitoring. For example, instead of saying "improve customer complaints regarding the laptop repair service," we may say "reduce customer complaints by 15 percent regarding the laptop repair service."
- A stands for *Assignable*, meaning that it must clearly identify a main process owner (or owners), responsible for both its deployment and proper functioning. For example, instead of saying "reduce customer complaints by 15 percent regarding the laptop repair service," we may add "which will be reported monthly by the laptop division manager and ultimately verified by the quality manager."
- R stands for *Realistic*, meaning that it cannot be pie in the sky. There's a huge difference between a declaration of intent and an achievable goal, and many managers mistake wishful thinking for disruptive and visionary planning. The feasibility of a corporate goal might be assessed based on available resources, past records or business standards. For example, "reducing customer complaints by 15 percent" sounds much more reasonable than "achieving 100 percent in customer acceptance."
- T stands for *Time-framed*, meaning that no objective is properly set if not given a specific time limit. This not only enables proper monitoring, but adds valuable information about the required dedication and feasibility of other related objectives (due to the overall amount of free resources). Hence, we shall say "reduce customer complaints by 15 percent regarding the laptop repair service by the end of this fiscal year" instead of "reduce customer complaints by 15 percent regarding the laptop repair service."

The importance of a proper definition of corporate goals is directly related to the feedback process depicted in Chapter 2 (Figure 2.2, step 6), and more precisely with the necessary process of revisiting defined strategies and matching its attained results with P&L and other performance indicators. Again, as mentioned at the beginning of this chapter, this stands as a key issue within the process of internal analysis. As such, we will be reviewing this in detail in Chapter 5.

Now that we have mastered the art of defining corporate goals, let's see what kind of weapons we have within our company with which to achieve them.

4.3 LEVERS FOR THE INTERNAL GENERATION OF VALUE

In order to influence the internal generation of value and achieve the fixed goals, a company may work in different fields through several actions and decisions. For example, a manager might decide to train the team in a specific skill, split a functional division into different working teams or launch a communication campaign to emphasize brand attributes. These applied actions taken under specific fields have a leverage effect on company performance, representing the main tangible tools to use and work on. Thus, we shall call them *levers*. Each one of these levers has a specific *focus* and ultimate *keystones* that define its scope and impact within an organization (Figure 4.3). The term lever is consciously used to indicate that, within its scope, an adequate appliance can have a significant impact on the generation of value through different ways. For example, a highly motivated and proactive taskforce with specific skills will stand as a differential factor for competition.

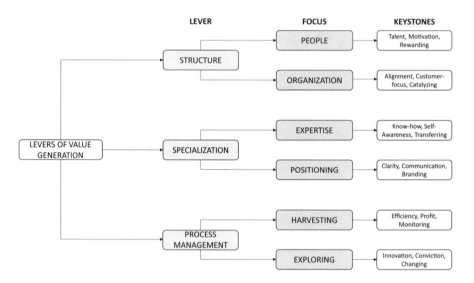

Figure 4.3   The levers for internal value generation

Therefore, and to further develop this assumption, the assessment of corporate levers for internal value generation is based on a three-level model (LIV, hereafter) consisting of the following elements:

- The *lever* itself. We may identify three of them:
  - The *Structure* lever deals with anything related to organizational design, corporate architecture, talent recruitment and staff empowerment. The basic premise here is that a talented and motivated taskforce, along with a corporate structure that accompanies and encourages its growth, is definitely a major asset for value generation.
  - The *Specialization* lever concerns the generation of a cross-company level of both strategic and operating excellence and know-how. This high degree of specialization shall lead the company not only to an operating excellence, but also to a brand positioning that enables and boosts value appreciation.

- The *Process Management* lever is concerned with every activity related to the conceptualization, planning, monitoring and execution of long-term corporate focus, scope and processes.
- The *focus*, understood as one the different scopes existing for a given lever. It not only defines a specific framework, but also helps to understand its areas of influence within a company and foreseeable outcomes.
- The *keystones* are the ultimate goals and motivations of the actions carried out under every given lever and specific focus.

The combination of lever, focus and keystone define a framework for specific actions taken in order to achieve a corporate goal. Some of these goals might require the combined effect of different actions, each one of them taken under a specific lever. To fully understand how the model works, let's have a step-by-step review of the structure for each lever and a further example of application.

4.3.1 Structure

The Structure lever encompasses two focuses:

1. *People*, concerning the human resources dimension and therefore the analysis of every action focused on how to recruit, retain, motivate, reward and empower the best possible taskforce according to the needs of the company's business and value model.
2. *Organization*, concerning the design of a customer-focused corporate architecture, aligned with the company goals and serving as an overall catalyzer for employee empowerment and value delivering.

4.3.2 Specialization

The Specialization lever encompasses two focuses as well:

1. *Expertise*, covering all activities related to the development of a specific internal know-how, as well as its transmission and sharing. Also, the raising of the collective awareness and acknowledgment of this know-how within the company. Expertise, from this point of view, is the ingoing focus of the Specialization lever.
2. *Positioning*, covering all activities that concern the creation of a solid, clear and differentiated brand personality based upon the value proposition. This involves all kind of communication and market-targeting actions. Positioning, from this point of view, is the outgoing focus of the Specialization lever.

4.3.3 Process Management

The Process Management lever encompasses two last focuses:

1. *Harvesting* covers all types of processes and activities targeting the operation of the conventional, well-known business within a company. These types of businesses are at a natural mature stage, and hence focused on profitability, efficiency and margin monitoring.
2. *Exploring* covers all types of processes and activities targeting the exploration of new, potential businesses, still in an uncertain and tentative stage and therefore focused on the long term, innovation and change management.

Applied Example: The Car Repair Shop

Sparkatronics[2] is a once-popular multi-brand chain of car repair shops spread all over the country. Its popularity has decreased, along with the profitability ratios, during the past few years. This has been primarily attributed to the fierce competition coming, on one hand, from the official OEM repairers (targeting brand-focused customers) and low-cost garages (targeting price-sensitive customers), on the other.

The company has recently undergone a major period of reflection and restructuring. As a result of it, the brand new managing board has decided to rethink the whole business model from scratch, using the TDV and internal value generation methodology. The final objective is to create an interconnected set of actions in order to accomplish the previously defined new corporate goals.

Once completed, the TDV methodology for the external analysis reveals the following results (summarized):

- As shown in Chart 4.1, car maintenance still accounts for 6.7–12.5 percent of total annual expenses regarding car ownership in mature markets. Thus, it is foreseeable that any improvement in this figure would stand as a major value deliverer for most customers.
- OEM's requirements regarding manufacturing processes, quality control and technology have been substantially increased during the last years. This increasing product complexity impacts bottom-line ratios for Sparkatronics.
- Some new vehicle segments (for example, electric cars and hybrids) lack a specialized network of repair shops.
- Located somewhere in between the official brand repairers and the low-cost garages, the company positioning has become blurred and uncertain. Neither brand lovers nor price-conscious customers (traditional segmentation) are really attracted by the value proposition.

---

2   Fictitious example for teaching purposes.

Annual car expenses in UK (as % of total cost)

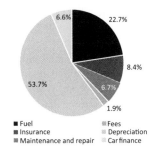

Annual car expenses in Spain (as % of total cost)

Annual car expenses in US (as % of total cost)

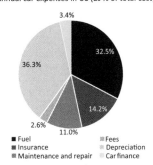

Chart 4.1   Annual car expenses in different countries
Source: Data from RAC 2010; Bureau of Labor Statistics 2010, Fleet Data 2012.

- The company's retail capillarity and coverage of territory is an important asset.
- Regarding customer insights:
  - Car repair and maintenance is widely considered a very expensive service through most customer segments;
  - Average lead time on car repair is considered too long—the time spent without car is considered a major problem;
  - Opening times and the appointment system are far too restrictive and non-customized;
  - The possibility of financing the cost of repair is a go/no-go criteria for a broad range of customer segments;
  - Multi-brand repair shops are perceived as cheaper, but less specialized options. Brand exclusivity adds quality perception and know-how to the mix of value;
  - Typical post-repair quality control checks, mainly based on long phone-based surveys, are perceived as a significant annoyance. SMS-based information and promotion systems, on the other hand, are equally perceived. In general terms, consumers consider that both types of processes add no value for them.

Based on these results, and under the approach of the LIV methodology, the Sparkatronics' managing board proposed a set of corporate goals, summarized in Table 4.1.[3] Moreover, each of these goals are to be accomplished by taking specific actions under the three available internal levers (Table 4.2). Note how a goal can be tackled through a set of actions concerning different levers. For example, the overall reduction of Average Delivery Time (goal B6) is approached from both the Expertise and the Harvesting focus. While the overarching angle is to further develop an already existing know-how, the idea is focusing both on the capacity of recording, transmitting and monitoring it (Expertise focus of the Specialization lever) and the continuous process improvement and efficiency (Harvesting Focus of the Process Management lever).

Table 4.1   Corporate goals by nature

A	Waiter Goals
1	Migrate strategic and operating business model from transactional to a relational one within a fiscal year

B	Cook Goals
2	Develop financial products for car maintenance expenses, conditional on the loyalty program membership
3	Reduce ASP by 15 percent per customer within two fiscal years
4	Move to a model-based specialization, instead of brand-base
5	Develop a specialization in electric and hybrid vehicles maintenance
6	Reduce average delivery time (ADT) by 25 percent in all car repairs within two fiscal years

C	Sweeper Goals
7	Design and deploy a customer-friendly quality control process within a fiscal year
8	Design and deploy an integrated process to undertake all bureaucratic workload concerning insurance companies
9	Design and deploy an integrated service to assist customers during the car repair process: replacement car
10	Extend and adapt cars' receiving and dispatching hours, according to customer's needs

---

3   Note that these goals are just a summary, and therefore lack a strict application of the SMART approach. A more detailed time-framed description and person in charge are missing from this example and should be present in a real case.

Table 4.2   Corporate goals by type of lever and focus

		A1	B2	B3	B4	B5	B6	C7	C8	C9	C10
Structure	People	x	x					x	x		
	Organization	x						x		x	x
Specialization	Expertise			x	x	x	x				x
	Positioning	x			x	x					
Process	Harvesting			x			x				
Management	Exploring	x				x					

Thus, an overview of the new Sparkatronics strategy reveals three main axes:

1. Move from an undifferentiated positioning to a specialization based on the car category. Every shop will have a specific specialization, according to the specific demand of its area. The categories are:
   - SUVs/Crossovers
   - Urban/Ultracompacts
   - Executive/Luxury
   - Family/Vans
   - Electric and Hybrid.
2. Migrate from a transactional to a relational customer approach. Leveraged on the existing channel dominance and brand recognition, this new model will be based on a renewable customer membership (covering annual maintenance and special conditions on stand-alone repairs) that will enable an overall price reduction, access to customized financing instruments, and a bureaucratic and accounting workload managing service.
3. Use this new framework to create a securitized customer basis and cash flow to further gain specialization, know-how and operating improvements. All this would eventually revert into a brand equity empowerment and clearer positioning.

The next logical step taken by the company is the accurate definition of the specific actions planned under each lever. Table 4.3 provides a sample of these actions for goals between B1 and B4. Note how important it is to ground the high-flying strategic guidelines resulting from the corporate shakedown: indeed, most of the problems of strategy definition typically arise during the execution stage. The managing board knows that the real added value comes from a flawless deployment!

It looks like everything is ready to roll for Sparkatronic. Are we missing anything? Yes: process monitoring and progress assessment. But this will be covered in Chapter 5: let's leave the company at this stage for the moment and focus on the next step within the internal analysis guidelines: the corporate positioning through the consolidation of a competitive model.

Table 4.3   Actions taken to accomplish corporate goals

Goal	Lever	Focus	Action
A1	Structure	People	• Recruit marketing experts • Recruit technological experts • Design and implement a comprehensive training suite for all employees • Promote key commercial to customer-segment leaders
		Organization	• Create a new marketing department to create an integrated customer-based relational model • Create a cross-company technology department to integrate customer relationship management (CRM) capabilities and software
	Process Management	Exploring	• Create a full-time taskforce to deliver the strategic guidelines of the new corporate taskforce • Define a new integrated process map with an overview of new requirements for the relational model • Define a market research methodology to map customer insights
	Specialization	Positioning	• Deploy a communication plan for the new brand positioning concerning the relational approach • Generate new positioning maps according to new brand attributes • Generate a briefing for strategic marketing positioning (customer + brand portfolio) to be internally distributed
B2	Structure	People	• Train financial staff to develop customized financial services and sustainable agreements with financial institutions • Train the commercial team to align the launching campaign with the new financial instruments

Goal	Lever	Focus	Action
B3	Specialization	Expertise	• Create a detailed cost-evaluation process for each type of car categories • Create a taskforce to standarize new purchasing, commercial and repair processes • Plan a operating staff relocation based on cost allocation results
	Process Management	Harvesting	• Evaluate supplier policy to push down average acquisition costs • Dimension a new price policy based on different growth scenarios for customer basis • Revaluate technical processes based on quality control, repair procedures and use of raw materials
B4	Specialization	Expertise	• Create a data warehouse collecting all know-how regarding car categories • Plan a operating staff relocation based on know-how specialization • Analyze geographic zone requirements to plan and develop a category-based shop network
	Specialization	Positioning	• Deploy a communication plan for the new brand positioning concerning the car-category specialization • Define an area-based customized communication plan to promote local shops
B5			

4.4 UNDERSTANDING COMPETITIVE MODELS: A DILEMMA

We started this chapter emphasizing the need for a value proposition to be easily identifiable as an unavoidable requirement in the way of success. In fact, a value proposition is nothing but the tangible representation of a competitive model from the customer perspective. In line with this, and as explained in Chapter 3 (Figure 3.3), linking a specific occasion of use to an emotion is the first step to build a loyalty link (relationship) between a customer and a brand. So far, we have approached this essential concept from the customer angle (value proposition, Figure 4.4), now it's time to look at it from the company one (competitive model). As we mentioned before, a clear understanding of the competitive model serves three major objectives:

1. Constitutes an internal benchmark for strategic guidelines;
2. Aligns internal resources toward a common goal;
3. Enables further market positioning and identifiable value proposition.

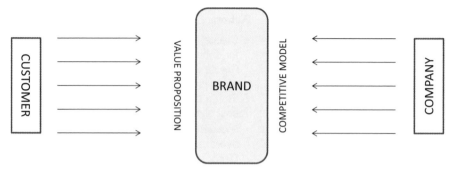

Figure 4.4   Different perspectives on the company/customer relationship

A common misconception about the creation of a competitive model lies in the belief that it must be clearly defined prior to any market research, customer target identification or any other market-driven activity, so that the corporate capabilities assessment and core competences definition should allegedly come in first place. In other words: this is what I can do best, now let's introduce it to the world to see if it fits. We shall refer to this as the value proposition versus competitive model dilemma. However reasonable it might sound, as leveraged on self-created areas of expertise, this mental framework is nothing but a replication of the traditional way of approaching businesses depicted in Figure 2.1 (Section 2.1), and hence definitely not a desirable way to face competition. Instead, the definition of a competitive model (as reported in Section 4.1.1) should come from the match of identified drivers of competitiveness, namely the outcome of the TDV model analysis and therefore the overall starting point, and the key corporate assets and capabilities. The difference between the two approaches is substantial, and based on three points:

1. The prevalence of value as it is understood by the customer over the company perspective (*what is required* over *what I can do best*).
2. The prioritizing of the capacity of the company to adapt to the competition requirements above any other matter, and therefore its potential readjustment of internal capabilities and expertise areas to better deliver what the business demands.
3. Based on the foregoing, the organic condition of every company, built on which it is able to encompass a consolidated area of expertise with its capacity to learn and evolve without betraying its value proposition.

It is, therefore, very important to demystify the so-called core competences of a company from the perspective of everlasting, sacrosanct principles to remain in the company forever. This doesn't mean that actions to develop a specific expertise or differential capability shouldn't be taken (in fact, the corporate levers are precisely intended for this), but simply that the spotlight should be focused on the market as the primary source of wealth: if the three dimensions of value are properly analyzed and understood, all further adaption in line with them is perfectly feasible. There are multiple examples of companies that have redefined their competitive model and product offering, along with its required operating capabilities, while remaining loyal to its essential value proposition and corporate culture:

- Nintendo, the Japanese video game giant, was founded as a playing card company in 1889.
- Nespresso, the operating unit of the Nestlé group manufacturing coffee capsules and coffee machines with an outstanding market share worldwide, was initially conceived and unsuccessfully launched in 1976 as a business to business (B2B) model for the hotel and catering industry, subsequently transformed into a business to consumer (B2C), retail-based experiential brand.
- National Geographic, a popular nonprofit scientific institution, moved from a pure publishing model to a multi-platform media brand to avoid a slow languish in its traditional distribution channel while remaining loyal to its foundational principles.
- IBM, initially a low-margin PC manufacturer, underwent a major structural shakedown to be reborn as an IT service provider.
- Ericsson, the Swedish company that held the leadership of the mobile phone business in 1997 (though just for a few months) to almost collapse a few years later, is currently the world leader in the mobile network infrastructure market.

The most iconic example, however of company transformation and core competence adaption might very well be Apple. As repeatedly addressed in previous chapters, back in 1996 Apple was a computer manufacturer and a niche player (Section 4.4.2 reviews its evolution in more detail). If we could travel in time and talk to an Apple board member in the early 2000s, he would probably be astonished to see the results of Chart 4.2, depicting the revenue distribution of the company by category for the first fiscal quarter of year 2014, and check how the Mac category accounts for little more than just 11 percent of the total revenue. Under this perspective, Apple is much more an online digital media store than a computer manufacturing company. Does this mean that Apple's value proposition has changed significantly from 2000? By no means. Regarding this, check what Tim Cook (currently Apple's formal CEO, but just acting CEO back then), stated during a conference with investors in 2009 (Go, 2011):

We believe that we are on the face of the earth to make great products and that's not changing. We are constantly focusing on innovating. We believe in the simple not the complex. We believe that we need to own and control the primary technologies behind the products that we make, and participate only in markets where we can make a significant contribution. We believe in saying no to thousands of projects, so that we can really focus on the few that are truly important and meaningful to us. We believe in deep collaboration and cross-pollination of our groups, which allow us to innovate in a way that others cannot. And frankly, we don't settle for anything less than excellence in every group in the company, and we have the self-honesty to admit when we're wrong and the courage to change. And I think regardless of who is in what job those values are so embedded in this company that Apple will do extremely well.

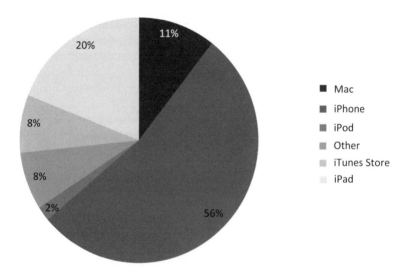

Chart 4.2   Apple's revenue by category (Q1 2014)
Source: Data from Apple Financial Report 1Q14 2014.

Note how these words could perfectly fit in a speech pronounced in both year 2000 or 2014 and the implications that this has regarding the competitive model-value proposition dilemma. A secondary question would be: Has Apple somehow modified some of its core capabilities, reinforced others and completely focused on new areas of expertise to keep its essential value proposition throughout the last 20 years? Most definitely.

Keeping in mind this permanent requirement for adaptation as a competitive precondition, it's extremely useful for start-ups and consolidated companies alike to understand the existing strategic and operating options behind different value propositions and the firmest competitive models successfully competing in a business. For the former, as a benchmark in its pursuit of an efficient competitive model, whereas for the latter, as a sort of a fill-in-the-gaps assessment procedure of its own competitive model and as a baseline for continuous improvement. But also, for both of them, of course, as an opportunity to challenge the conventional status quo and innovate on the basis of a disruptive value proposition. This is the reason why we will be focusing on the competitive model assessment in the following sections.

4.4.1 Competitive Priorities

The concept of competitive priority originally arises from manufacturing companies, while dimensioning and planning operating processes according to available resources, machinery workload, and inbound and outbound logistics (Hayes and Wheelwright, 1984), to further evolve into a cross-industry approach to business competition, partially due to the late influence of Michael Porter's prior classic *Competitive Strategy: Techniques for Analyzing Industries and Competitors* (1980) where he introduced the core aspects of differentiation strategy.

As an academic definition, competitive priorities address the objectives and the scope of an organization, covering different operating aspects and defining an overarching approach to competition. To put it in simpler terms, a competitive priority is *a specific expertise that stands as a differential feature of the company and a cross-operating guideline for all the organization*. As such, a competitive priority must be acknowledged, shared and deployed by all business agents (employees, suppliers, managing board). It must be understood as a corporate manifesto, an unbreakable commitment with the customer.

On the other hand, and despite the thorough literature existing in this field and the relatively diverse array of competitive priorities identified, most of them are indeed redundant and a mere combination of the five basic types, namely *Cost*, *Quality*, *Innovation*, *Flexibility* and *Service*. Table 4.4 gathers a detailed explanation for each one, together with the corresponding operating focus to reach it.

Table 4.4   The five competitive priorities

Competitive Priority	Definition	Operating Focus
Cost	• Production and distribution at low cost (compared to average)	• Scale economies • Value chain optimization
Quality	• Reliable and flawless products • Performance standards • Conformance to specifications • Durability	• Process and product control
Service	• Customization (experience) • Ability to accompany the customer throughout the business process • Capacity to engage and involve the customer in the value-creation process	• Customer Relationship Management
Innovation	• New or improved solutions and products delivered on a regular basis • Ability to change operating or strategic business drivers	• Applied R&D
Flexibility	• Ability to handle changes in changes and product mix • Reliable and fast delivery • Customization (product or service variety, number of products)	• Lead time control • Time-to-market

Although not always, these competitive priorities are usually combined to create a more complex competitive model, partly because this leads to stronger competitive advantages and partly because, just as it happens in any other living ecosystem, dominant business models create dominant players, and, as such, endure in time. The consolidation of competitive models is a key issue within the process of internal analysis. As such, we will be reviewing this in detail in Chapter 5.

On the other hand, and despite the different existing angles and nomenclature (such as Porter's generic strategies, for example, that consider cost leadership and differentiation strategy separately), the underlying concept behind the competitive priorities approach is that any given organization generates value through a *specialization* in a specific area that enables a *differentiation* process through a public *Positioning*. As explained repeatedly in Chapter 3, this differentiation is absolutely key in order to be competitive, and this is why we considered (as depicted in Figure 4.4), the value proposition to be nothing but the tangible delivery of a solid competitive model. The extent to which this specialization can be sustained, appreciated and understood by its customers will critically condition the competitiveness of an organization.

From a B2C perspective, customers can easily identify these diverse competitive priorities for a given set of competitors operating in a specific market, even if they are unaware of it. Companies themselves reinforce this perception by using competitive priorities as a tool for communication. Why? Because it works. Take a look at some examples of real taglines used by well-known companies presented in Table 4.5.

Table 4.5   Some examples on company positioning

Company	Sector	Tagline	Highlight
Wal-Mart	Consumer goods	*Save money. Live better*	Cost
Southwest Airlines	Airline	*Low fares. NO hidden Fees*	Cost
APC	Electrical components	*Legendary reliability*	Quality
Bank of America	Financial services	*Higher standards*	Quality
Panasonic	Technology	*Slightly ahead of its time*	Innovation
Hewlett-Packard	Technology	*Invent*	Innovation
Morgan Stanley	Financial services	*One client at a time*	Service
Greyhound	Travel services	*Leave the driving to us*	Service
Burger King	Restaurants	*Have it your way*	Flexibility
Zurich	Insurance	*Because change happenz*	Flexibility

Obviously, these are just examples. On many other occasions it's not possible to draw such a clear parallelism. Sometimes the message is not aiming to clarify its positioning, but trying to generate awareness (for example, Cialis: "Will you be ready?"), identify the target group (for example, Mutual of America: "Your retirement company") or associate positive feelings (for example, Nissan: "Enjoy the ride"). Sometimes the message is simply unintelligible for ordinary mortals (for example, Lucent Technologies: "Creating value through convergence").

Be that as it may, most communication efforts are unarguably focused on highlighting a specialization and, more than anything, making a promise to the customer that could be understood and appreciated. Remember: simplifying and clarifying your value proposition will take you half the way toward success.

4.4.2 Competitive Models: Positioning

When it comes to elements of competitive positioning, and to make an understandable parallelism, we might say that *priorities* are to *models* what the heart and blood vessels are to the circulatory system: components that are clearly identifiable and important separately, but acquire their real value as part of a more complex system.

Indeed, based on the harnessing of operating synergies, companies might combine different expertise (competitive priorities) to generate a more complex approach to competition that has an identity in itself: a competitive model. For example, the Spanish company Inditex (the world's largest clothing retailer), uses its ability to handle lead times and adapt to changes in demand (*Flexibility*), together with its superior control over logistics and manufacturing processes (*Quality*) to penetrate a great number of customer segments, and hence generate a significant cash flow. Along with other aspects of its strategy (such as its particular marketing approach and a very aggressive retail policy, among other others), this allows Inditex to keep prices low at its Zara shops (*Cost*) and hence reinvest this dramatic liquidity in the optimization of the model. The Zara (Inditex) competitive model, therefore, is based on an accurate use of the different synergies generated through its different competitive priorities (see Section 4.4.3 for an accurate description of Inditex's model).

An important aspect to highlight is that the different competitive models are usually adopted by business contenders with regards to their respective dominance and target group. Based on both drivers, we may identify two types of contenders:

- *Mass marketers* target a very large number of customers, leveraging their channel dominance to deliver a cross-segment value proposition. Note how this is most frequently associated to big companies, as the access to scale economies and the position of power in relation to the distribution channel are typically knock-out requirements.
- *Niche players* target a specific, restricted group of customers leveraging their specialization to deliver a customized value proposition. These types of contenders usually translate this specialization into either higher unitary margins or segment exclusivity (serving a vast majority of existing customers within a given segment or market niche). A common misconception about niche players is to ascribe to them small or local markets and parochial competitive approaches, whereas this might be true just in some specific cases. Niche players might very well be global, as long as their market niches are global as well. However, although a niche player's business model can be perfectly solid, it may become instable in some specific scenarios. Should their value proposition become increasingly popular, niche players naturally tend to adopt a mass marketer approach to business (cost optimization, product standardization, channel dominance or massive brand exposure) while trying to keep some sense of exclusivity and customization from the original value proposition (this is what happened, for example, with Apple). These two conflicting approaches, needless to say, are typically hard to combine and may result in an increasingly confusing value proposition (Apple, however, has handled this situation pretty well, as explained in Chapter 3).

On the other hand, and differently than competitive priorities (which are basically reduced to the options mentioned in the previous chapter), the number of potential business models cannot be delimited, due to the fact that the number of potential synergies and the specific nuances of their application enable (at least, from a theoretical perspective) multiple potential competitive models. All in all, these are good news: it would be really boring to be part of a business environment in which all ways of competition have already been invented!

However, in spite of this seemingly unlimited number of options, the number of competitive models eventually used by successful companies is, in fact, quite limited (check Figure 4.5). The conclusions about this are twofold:

1. On one hand, it shows that they actually work (again, at this point we note a natural selection perspective). Business success is quite often linked to reliability and robustness and, precisely for that reason, consolidated competitive models are taken as benchmarks and approached as a basis upon which to build. It is, therefore, very likely that certain common patterns can be identified in any competitive scenario. In other words: working on the basis of a well-known, solid and identifiable business model is part of the value delivery itself.

2. On another hand, the combination of different competitive priorities, if mastered, tend to generate synergies that further enable a consolidated position of power for a company that would be very hard to achieve any other way. This basically means that, in any given competitive scenario, and until no disruptive innovation (such as a major technological breakthrough or a completely new proposition of value) modifies its current paradigm, the potential ways in which a company can be profitable are pretty limited, and therefore it is very likely to identify and group the different business contenders based on them. Anyway, this applies to the *conceptualization* of the business model from a global perspective: of course, the key added value lies within the capacity to ground this theoretical model and deliver superior value to the customer while mastering operational excellence. Just because every single CEO in the food and beverage industry understands Coke's competitive model, for example, it doesn't mean that they are able to bring their company to its level!

It is, therefore, highly recommendable to review the most salient and credible competitive models in order to understand the different paths for business success. Whether this knowledge should be used by a new contender to try to replicate or rather challenge them, is something that the reader must decide.

Be that as it may, Figure 4.5 depicts the most salient competitive models, together with the type of business contender typically adopting it, based on the combination of competitive priorities leading to their constitution. Let's review them carefully using some practical examples.

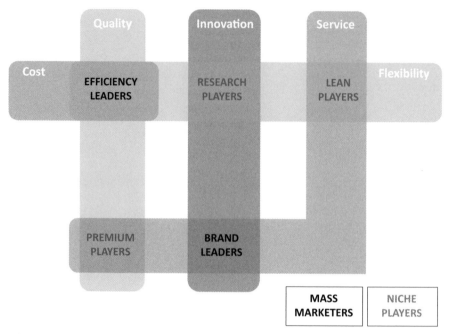

Figure 4.5   Most salient competitive models

4.4.3 Efficiency Leaders

In every given business, there's always a contender offering a price-sensitive value proposition, typically leveraged on a very aggressive cost structure (by aggressive we understand its capacity to cut costs along the entire value chain). In terms of competitive priorities, these types of contenders are focused on *costs*. Although this might result in a successful strategy, and as we have already mentioned in previous chapters, a mere cost competition unfailingly leads to a commoditization of the value proposition, a price war and a subsequent margin predation.

Compared to this, a dominant mass marketer might leverage its position of power based on a more complex competitive model (as we explained in Section 4.4.2). This competitive model is deeply related to cost control and price competition but also combined with an impressive capacity to deliver a sustained excellence in terms of operating and manufacturing capabilities (product and process control, namely Quality) and an outstanding capacity to quickly adapt to changes in customer preferences (Flexibility). We shall refer to these types of mass marketers as *Efficiency Leaders*.

Note how the Cost and Flexibility dimensions are typically subject to trade-offs, as Flexibility normally demands resource-intensive processes (by deploying more highly skilled workers or general purpose manufacturing processes instead of more efficient ones, for example). Therefore, those companies able to encompass both of them in a coherent value proposition are not frequent and largely dominant.

The degree to which an Efficiency Leader is more focused on Cost, Flexibility or Quality varies from case to case, and pretty much depends on the business or industry requirements. Each one of them creates a differential value proposition that might very well be unique (in the end, this is why they are successful), but it is completely feasible to find common patterns and similar baselines between them.

The traditional way the Efficiency Leader competitive model works is as follows:

- Leveraging an outstanding operating capability (logistics, manufacturing, distribution, supplier control) and its capacity to standardize and control it (Quality), the company is able to outperform business standards.
- A full control and constant monitoring over the entire value chain, typically combined with a smart dimensioning of the organizational structure that boosts customer focus (efficient leaders, just like any successful company, are customer-focused), allow the company to significantly reduce time-to-market and lead time. The capacity to quickly grasp and understand changes in customer preferences from a cross-perspective, combined with a reduced time-to-market (Flexibility) enables a major competitive advantage and, hence, a quick market penetration.
- This market penetration has both cause and effect implications for a dominant channel presence and very aggressive retail policy (where appropriate), thus quickly consolidating as a business benchmark and a top-of-mind reference for a wide array of customers.
- The combination of value chain control, global presence and outstanding operating capabilities result in economies of scale and substantial cost-cutting procedures (Cost).

In conclusion, note that there are two key drivers to understand how the competitive model of an Efficiency Leader is triggered: on one hand, a customer-focused organization, with a flexible, market-driven structure and reduced time-to-market. On the other, a sustained operating excellence. As you can easily imagine, this is a devastating combination (for competitors, of course). In fact, to the extent that they are solid enough, Efficiency Leaders business models lead to the emergence of extremely dominant contenders, frequently with an undisputed market space.

Some examples of Efficiency Leaders in different business are Inditex, Wal-Mart or Ikea, among others. Despite the fact that they show some differences (Inditex is best known for its flexibility, Wal-Mart for its low prices and Ikea for a combination of both), their competitive models share common roots.

Applied Example: Inditex

In 2013, Inditex sales exceeded 23 billion dollars worldwide, accounting for an accumulated growth of more than 21 percent during the period 2011–13 and consolidating its position as the biggest fashion group in the world. The Inditex group operates over 6,300 stores in 87 countries, and owns eight different brands: Zara, Pull&Bear, Massimo Dutti, Bershka, Stradivarius, Oysho, Zara Home and Utterque. They all share a common commercial and managerial approach, while the group operates in the low-cost and outlet segment through its brand Lefties (although there is no reference of the Inditex group anywhere on its website or in its stores). Among them, Zara stands out as the most important and well-known brand, accounting for more than 68 percent of Inditex's global sales and 14 percent of market share in Spain.

Chart 4.3 depicts a comparison of some key metrics in the fashion retail business for diverse contenders. Gap (an American retailer) and H&M (Swedish) are among Inditex's traditional competitors, whereas Prada (Italian) is a pure Premium Player (we'll get to that a bit further). Gap, H&M and Inditex's competitive models, despite their differences, do have solid resemblances and might be assessed on a relatively equal basis in order to understand Inditex's excellence. Prada, in turn, might be used as a benchmark to understand a different positioning in the same business.

Inditex's global sales have been between 14–20 percent higher than H&M's (probably, its fiercest competitor) during the last three years. This difference is much bigger if we compare it with Gap (between 31 percent and 43 percent). Of course, this difference is massive in the case of Prada, but this is not a fair comparison: Prada is not a mass marketer, but a niche player, and therefore the sales volume alone does not reflect the reality of their respective competitive performance. Note how, as explained before, higher volumes of sales do involve easier access to economies of scales.

A quick glimpse into their respective gross margin metrics reveals a major difference in terms of operating efficiency between Inditex and H&M, on the one hand, and Gap, on the other: the former are able to keep their cost of sales significantly below the latter (around 10 percent, on average). This is further confirmed by comparing their operating margins (that is to say, including all operating expenses): albeit Inditex is performing better than H&M, the true difference is appreciated upon comparing it with Gap (between 4 percent and 8 percent lower for Gap). This metric is key because it provides information about how efficient the company sales are. For a mass marketer, increasing sales while keeping operating margin high is a clear (and rare) sign of a cross-value proposition that is able to seduce a wide array of customer segments, combined with an ability to do it in a very efficient way.

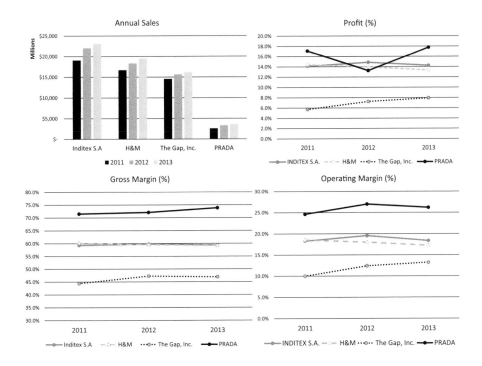

Chart 4.3   A comparison of key metrics for the fashion retail business
Source: Data from Bloomberg Businessweek, 2014a, b, c, d.

The case of Prada, in turn, is very different: as explained in Section 4.4.2, a niche player is focused on higher unitary margins (see the difference in terms of both gross and operating margin for Prada and the rest of the contenders) but lower volume sales. The very same pattern might be found concerning the different profit metrics for the four companies.

Be that as it may, Inditex is doing significantly better than most of its competitors and quite better than H&M in terms of operating capabilities. The explanation can be found in its legendary logistics excellence. But there are other reasons. Inditex's marketing costs, for example, represents 0.3 percent of sales, compared to an average 3–4 percent in its industry (Inditex has very little above-the-line advertising, and never on TV or radio). On the other hand, it takes 15 days on average to turn a new design idea into a finished product delivered to the stores. In the case of H&M, it takes from three to five months. An extremely short time to market!

Operating excellence is, as we already know, a key requirement in the competitive model of an Efficiency Leader. But it is not the only one. What can we say about its Flexibility and customer-focused dimensioning? Well, on average, unsold items account for less than 10 percent of stock (compared to 17–20 percent of industry average). More than 85 percent of the items are sold at full price, which is 15–20 percent higher than the industry average. Inditex very much reinforces quick and *take-it-or-lose-it* sales, leveraged on its more than 40,000 new designs per year. Inditex customers do know that they had better buy the item the first time they see it as it is very likely to be gone by the next time they come back to the store. This is, by the way, very frequent: an average customer visits the group's stores 17 times per year (compared with four times for its main competitors). Retailers, for their part, are allowed to change 40–50 percent of their orders once the season has started (thus avoiding overproduction). All in all, everything in Inditex moves around a fast adaptation to customer preferences! In fact, in 2006, Inditex's main goal was announced to be: "to get the shortest time to market and to get the lowest time of response to consumers:" a clear declaration of intentions.

In conclusion: Inditex is a strong and paradigmatic Efficiency Leader. H&M is another one, slightly different in some aspects but very much based on the same competitive model. However, Inditex is simply doing better: selling more, at a higher unitary margin, with an extended retail presence, a faster market response and higher market share. A definitive evidence of this might be found in the different share values depicted in Chart 4.4. It looks like Inditex is really able to understand how value is appreciated and transmitted in its business.

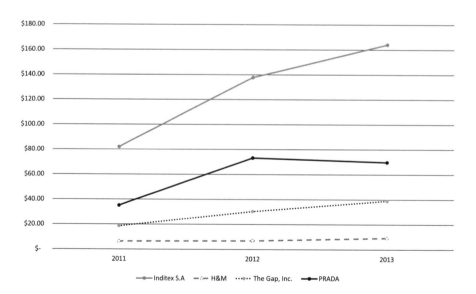

Chart 4.4   Different share values within the fashion retail business
Source: Data from Bloomberg Businessweek 2014a, b, c, d.

Applied Example: IKEA

Defining Ikea's business approach is not trivial. To begin with, Ikea is the world's largest furniture chain. In 2013, the group sales exceeded 39 billion dollars worldwide. But Ikea is not a simple furniture maker (the company is now selling solar panels in its UK stores, for example). Its business concept incorporates a mixture of different traces from others, turning it into a paradigmatic example of the blue ocean theory (see Section 2.1, and try to think of a global competitor for IKEA: you won't find any). Think of it: traditional furniture makers normally have a clear specialization (home or office furniture, premium design or low-cost clonals and so on), sell their products assembled, deliver them to the home and leverage their growth in a design-based and frequently urban retail policy (own stores or third-party distributors). Consequently, their figures typically reflect heavy cost structures, both linked to overheads (mainly production facilities, taskforce and logistics) and purchasing costs.

Ikea's customers, in turn, self-assemble their furniture, pick it up and take it home, all by themselves. The company has no fashion-designed retail shops or even distribution agreements with third parties, but just mega stores located on the outskirts of most medium to large cities around the world. The number of in-store sales assistants is openly (and intentionally) insufficient, whereas furniture transportation and assembly are ancillary services that IKEA outsources to external companies and for which customers, needless to say, must pay separately. Even the furniture pickup at the massive store warehouses is either to be assumed by the customer or paid for separately! This somehow resembles other operating models from different businesses, such as Ryanair, in which a core, naked product or service is delivered at a reduced price, while any other service is considered an add-on (yet available). Despite what it may seem, the key success factor is not the price, but the *Flexibility*: the capacity to understand the trade-off between price and service, design and comfort that the customer is willing to accept.

Indeed, although it might sound a bit aggressive (compared with the traditional approach of furniture makers) this do-it-yourself (DIY) approach has proved extremely successful, and yet a brilliant example of how to redefine a conventional value proposition by reassessing what customers really want and are willing to pay for (Appreciation dimension of value) and subsequently eliminating the stages within the value chain and purchasing process that are nothing but predating value to focus on how to really boost it (Concentration). Ikea's vision, as officially stated, is *to create a better everyday life for the many people.* No mention of furniture anywhere.

But this is just one of the three pillars of the Efficiency Leader business model in the Ikea case: Flexibility. Let's see how they leverage its growth on the other two, deeply related with its operating excellence: *Quality* and *Cost*.

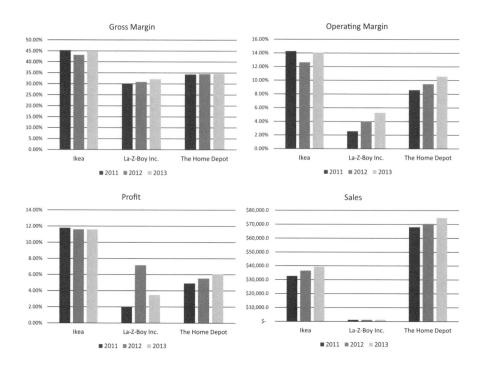

Chart 4.5   A comparison of key metrics for the furniture and DIY business

Source: Data from Bloomberg Businessweek, 2014e, f; IKEA Yearly Summary (2010–13).

As previously mentioned, IKEA's business model cannot be compared with other furniture makers solely, as it includes aspects of others like the DIY one. Of course, a company's set of competitors are much better identified by assessing similar value propositions (therefore, benefits expected by the customer and occasion of use/purchase) rather than by looking within the boundaries of its same sector (you may want to review the applied example about surfing in Australia in Chapter 3 at this point). Differently to the Inditex example, IKEA simply has no comparable competitor, so we may look at the figures of leading companies within both the furniture and the DIY businesses in an attempt to have a fairer comparison. You can check the results on Chart 4.5.

There have been different attempts to name Ikea's business. One of the most consolidated ones is *indoor living*, despite the fact that this fails to fully grasp its intended area of influence within their customers' life (as this would not include outdoor decoration or gardening, which are important store departments). Be that as it may, and in the absence of a better one, we will use it. As the US stands as one of top-selling countries for IKEA (see Chart 4.6), accounting for 12 percent of the company's global sales (despite its small market share), we shall use the examples of other US major competitors for the furniture making business (La-Z-Boy) and DIY business (Home Depot).

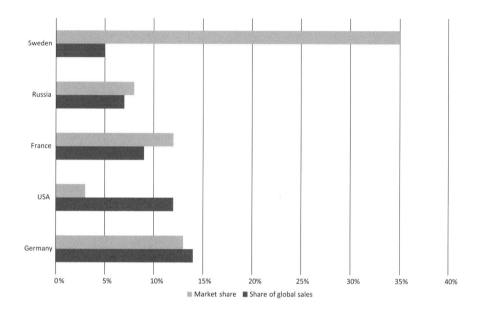

Chart 4.6   Ikea's top five selling countries
Source: Data from EuroMonitor, 2013.

Home improvement (including here the DIY sub-business) is a massive business, and Home Depot (HD) undoubtedly its most salient contender. Its global sales roughly double Ikea's, although basically leveraged on its US market dominance (11.70 percent market share). HD has 2,256 stores in the US, Canada and Mexico. However, from Ikea's point of view, it's basically a local competitor. The Swedish giant has 301 stores in 41 countries, with a growing market share in each and every one of them (see Chart 4.6), this being a defining feature of Efficiency Leaders.

The same applies to La-Z-Boy (LZB), a US-based local competitor (312 stores, but just 93 company owned) in the furniture making business, with overall sales representing a bit more than 3 percent of Ikea's global figures but with a bigger US market share (around 5 percent). LZB is the most recognized name in the furniture industry and the world's leading reclining chair manufacturer.

Despite its differences in market share (though rapidly changing) and a difficult comparison in terms of sales volume, Ikea beats both HD and LZB in every single metric, revealing a superior operating excellence and a massively improved bottom line (Chart 4.5). This efficiency is shown in the gross margin (between 10–12 percent bigger than HD's and LZB's), the operating margin (9–10 percent bigger) and profit (5–8 percent bigger) ratios. There are several operating factors that explain this:

- Ikea excels at implementing economics of scale, standardizing most raw materials and components and using self-assembled products to reduce operational and delivery costs.
- The company internalizes the manufacturing and distribution of the raw materials accounting for the most significant part of the cost of sales (and most frequently used components) through two different groups that control the entire value chain: Swedwood and Swedspan. As of September 1, 2013, they were both rebranded under the common name of Ikea Industry. This new organization controls the entire value chain of all wood-based components, from the management and connection with forests operations to all furniture production.
- All Ikea products are flat-packed, optimizing stock and transportation procedures and allowing an easier pick-up by the customers at the store warehouses. Besides, 58 percent of suppliers deliver directly to stores, hence reducing even further the logistic costs. Transportation costs in 2013 and 2012 were lower than the previous year.
- Other cost-saving procedures come from *recycling* (broken in-store packaging, customers donations, among others), *waste reduction, re-selling* of returns and damaged products at lower prices, *corporate thriftiness* (stores encourage and reward employees to reduce overall energy consumption) and *strategic placement* of stores (located in high-density zones to guarantee store traffic and ensure visibility from highways or important roads).
- Despite its wide product range (consisting of 9,500 products, with 2,000 new ones being launched every year, conceptualized by 12 in-house designers and 60–70 external designers), typically associated with bigger unitary prices, Ikea lowered average product prices (already much lower than competitors') by 0.2 percent in 2013.

In conclusion, Ikea has simply blown away all competition by offering affordable design at a lower price within a flexible, market-driven and agile value proposition that comes along with a substantial cost-reduction leveraged by an outstanding operating excellence. Piece of cake, right?

4.4.4 Brand Leaders

We've been reviewing how Efficiency Leaders base their success on a cross-value proposition to target as many customers as possible by delivering a highly adaptable value proposition at a very affordable price.

In contrast with them, other mass marketers within a given business move toward a more aspirational positioning, in which the company brand stops being perceived as a *convenient benchmark* to turn into a *desired benchmark*. This is a major difference that consequently comes along with a totally different competitive model. From the Appreciation perspective, note how the value proposition is totally different. Despite their blatant success, it is certainly difficult to imagine anyone madly rushing into an IKEA store or a Zara shop, eager to buy a Hemnes bookcase or a 20-dollar shirt. However, we are all familiar with the image of endless queues in front of Apple stores before the launching of a new i-gadget or with the idea of some kid saving for months to buy a pair of Nike Air Max.

These mass marketers adopt a *Brand Leader* business model, based on a combination of *Innovation* and *Service*. Companies like Apple, Nike, Sony or SAP, amongst many others, are good representatives of this competitive model.

Compared to Efficiency Leaders, Brand Leaders trade-off Price for Innovation and Flexibility for Service. This is a key aspect, as long as average customers are willing to pay more to obtain a bigger share of value (we already know that) within the limits of their acquisition power. However, justifying a bigger price in a bloodthirsty, crowded business is very hard to do. It is important to note that, differently to Premium Players (we'll be reviewing them in Section 4.4.7), who typically target non-price-sensitive segments and therefore might be much more based on intangible attributes and leveraged mainly by Service, Brand Leaders target a wide customer basis (including those with high price sensitivity and those permanently based on a comparative feature analysis) and therefore must justify its higher price based on undisputedly solid and tangible arguments. A very solid way of doing so is by constantly delivering new or improved products: Innovation.

Thus, Brand Leaders undertake the commitment of delivering Innovation on a regular basis as the real driver for their success, while keeping an important, yet secondary focus on Service as an entry barrier to distance themselves even further from specific Efficiency Leaders and reinforce brand loyalty. Take Apple, for example: the company has based its great success on the constant delivery of innovative technologic devices. This is what Apple does, this is what their customers expect from them: new products, new devices, new solutions. In the computer hardware business, however, the urge for Innovation is probably even more acute than in most others, so that almost every contender is also trying to deliver innovative solutions. This constant pressure for fast-moving, innovative devices, if not addressed, shortens product lifecycles and impacts global profitability. A complementary focus on Service (customization, customer care) serves as a differentiation tool to strengthen the customer-brand link and thus reinforce loyalty attitudes. In the case of Apple, Service is delivered in different ways, such as the exclusive training package in iOS-based devices to be purchased exclusively at its official stores and simultaneously with a new device, through the AppleCare service (tech support, maintenance, insurance, warranty extension and so on), the own existence of the awesome Apple Stores and, of course, through the customization delivered by the platform for iOS-based mobile applications, AppStore.

Sony, for its part, has developed a digital platform for its PlayStation systems users, PlayStation Store, to offer exclusive downloadable contents, games extensions and online gaming. Moreover, the PlayStation Plus membership is advertised as a way to "get amazing features and benefits on PS4, PS3 and PS Vita systems"[4] and, by the way, used to create a soft captive market. All in all, community creation, sense of belonging and the fight for loyalty are the common hobbyhorses.

The Brand Leader model, of course, is not exclusive to the technology business (in which Innovation is easily understood as a key driver). Let's examine a different example.

Applied Example: Nike

Nike Inc. is undoubtedly the most famous and popular sport apparel and equipment manufacturer worldwide. In 2013 the company sales exceeded $25 billion, almost 27 percent higher than its main competitor, Adidas (see Chart 4.7), and more than six times higher than Puma, another key contender in the global business.

Nike is a clear example of a Brand Leader competitive model. Beginning with its mission statement ("To bring inspiration and innovation to every athlete"), the company has always shown a clear focus on Innovation as the main competitive priority. There are solid evidences to sustain it: while no official data about its R&D spending is available, Macquarie Capital estimates it at an average 5–9 percent of the group total sales (Cheng, 2014). Adidas, in turn, devotes less than 1 percent of its annual sales to R&D activities, and Puma 2.7 percent (Joint Research Center, 2012).

Furthermore, Nike has registered an overwhelmingly larger number of patents during the past 40 years, compared to both Adidas and Puma again (Chart 4.8). This superior Innovation focus results in much better profitability, as shown by comparing their respective five-year average return on equity ratio (Chart 4.8 again).

---

4   Sony Entertainment Network. "PlayStation Store". Available from: http://www.sony entertainmentnetwork.com/en-no/psstore/ [Accessed February 5, 2014].

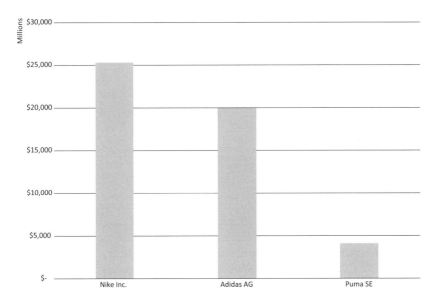

Chart 4.7   2013 sales for some sport apparel manufacturers (in millions of dollars)

Source: Data from Bloomberg Businessweek, 2014g, h, i.

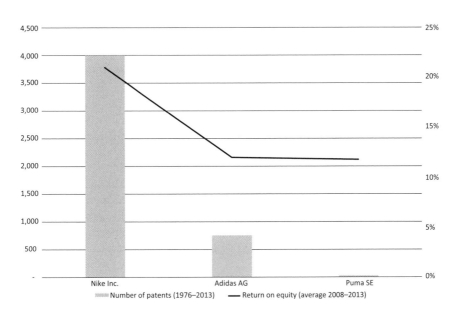

Chart 4.8   Innovation and profitability metrics for some sport apparel manufacturers

Source: Data from Bloomberg Businessweek, 2014; Cheng, 2014, Patents by Assignee Puma, n.d.

Moreover, and contrary to what might appear to be the case, the company has shown a clear evolution in corporate focus that very much reflects a rethinking in terms of how Nike can deliver value to its huge customer base (Innovation to the core). Indeed, Nike is today a different company from the one it used to be just ten years ago. In line with the idea explained in Chapters 2 and 3 about the need to be focused on the benefit delivered to the customer (sport experience and related feelings), instead of remaining anchored to a traditional product portfolio (sport apparel), in 2013 less than 50 percent of the 540 patents registered by Nike were related to footwear. Prior to the recession (2006), this percentage exceeded 75 percent.

Thus, in 2010, Nike created the Digital Sport Division. In less than four years, the company has transformed itself into a digital force, in yet another brilliant proof of how to understand the evolution in customers' Appreciation of Value. As the company expanded its product portfolio into fitness-tracking gadgets, devices like the 2012 FuelBand (an electronic bracelet that lets users track activity with simple color cues), or co-branding ventures like the one established with Apple in 2006 (joining Nike shoes and iPods to enhance the running experience and fitness tracking) significantly contributed to consolidate Nike's clear positioning as a true innovative company. More Innovation? However incredible it might seem, Nike is actually making *Back to Future II* (1989) film fans' dream a reality: in 2015, the company will be launching the celebrated self-lacing Nike shoes (Back to the future power laces, 2014) that Marty McFly (the film's main character) wore in an imaginary future ... set in 2015!

It's very important to highlight how, similar to Sony's approach, Innovation is also used by Nike to reinforce its Service Focus and strengthen the brand community creation: the NikePlus platform conveys all the information gathered by an exclusive Mobile App, tracked by devices like the SportWatch GPS (or the iPod, as explained) and displayed by the FuelBand, hence closing the circle in terms of fitness tracking experience for the user.

In terms of other remarkable services provided, the NikeiD program offers the possibility to create a unique pair of Nike shoes by customizing a base model. This includes color selection, specific shoe features and, of course, printing an eight-character text on either the heel or both sides of the shoes. Customization, as explained in Section 4.4.1 (Table 4.4) plays a major role when it comes to stress the Service Focus.

4.4.5 Research Players

Compared to mass marketers, the competition rules for niche players are totally different. Their tailor-made value propositions are restricted to very specific customer segments, and this entails pros and cons alike. Among the former, a restricted target normally enables a clearer focus and, consequently, a simplified and straightforward value proposition (on paper, it's much more simple to be appealing to a specific, reduced group of customers sharing common traits than to offer something that almost everyone likes). Moreover, a niche players' approach might correspond (though not necessarily) to smaller companies with lighter organizational structures better connected to market preferences that allow more flexible approaches.

On the other hand, niche players might deal (although not all of them, Premium Players normally don't) with an insufficient customer basis that makes the access to scale economies difficult and causes liquidity problems. Furthermore, a comparatively reduced financial muscle typically compromises their investing capacity, leaving them in a weakened position (again, this rarely applies to Premium Players).

As explained in Section 4.4.2, many successful niche players leverage their growth in either higher unitary margins (such as depicted in the Inditex example when referring to Prada) or segment exclusivity). However, some others have unstable competitive models. This does not necessarily have negative connotations, but simply means that they are not intended to last over time (although might also be considered successful).

Within this last category, Research Players are a good example. Their competitive model is a combination of Innovation and Flexibility, and typically correspond to small to medium companies offering (or developing) highly specific and innovative solutions either in B2B or B2C environments and very frequently (though not exclusively) linked to tech-based business. This value proposition traditionally involves a disruptive approach to new customer demands or the capacity to adapt to changes unable to be adopted by bigger, slower, non-flexible competitors. Start-ups and spin-offs, created upon a new product concept or an optimized process, are typical fits for this competitive model.

Research Players are unstable by their very nature, and by that we mean that just one stage within the company lifecycle. Their expected evolution ends up with three possible options:

1. Be acquired by a mass marketer or Premium Players

Some types of innovations are particularly hard or very unlikely to be developed by big, consolidated companies. One reason might be because they would require a very specific know-how or a high degree of specialization simply out of the reach of the company. Another possibility would be that, despite being potentially successful, these sort of innovations are out of the company's current scope or in direct opposition to their product portfolio, so would never be generated from within. Finally, a last explanation could be because of the company's overconfidence, resulting in a loss of contact with the market reality and therefore a lackadaisical attitude toward new approaches to competition.

Whatever the reason, the truth is that Research Players, typically small and medium enterprises (SMEs) with a much higher risk tolerance, do have much stronger incentives to undertake the development of such innovations. On the other hand, once it is consolidated enough (either from the product or market perspective) to be reckoned with, it's normally much more profitable for a bigger, more powerful company to immediately incorporate the innovation into its portfolio by directly acquiring the Research Player that has developed it, rather than to risk trying to develop a similar innovation by itself (in this case it would be dealing with longer time-to-market and, in any case, uncertain results). A buyout results not only in gaining an important competitive advantage (an increased channel presence, an improved product or an outstanding new capability), but also instantly eliminates a potential competitor.

The benefits are also important from the Research Player perspective—first and foremost because of the economic compensation. It is important to understand, however, that often the alternative option to selling the company is simply to not exist. That is to say: the company was born to be sold and selling it is the best option. Among the many examples of this, we may mention the acquisition of Android by Google (2005), Fundamo by VISA (2011) or Embark by Apple (2013).

However, the founders of some Research Players refuse to accept this and keep fighting a war that most likely they can't win … because they can't, right?

2. Disappear

This is definitely a plausible alternative to selling the company. Given the situation of competitive oligarchy existing in many business, the chances for a Research Player to confront much bigger companies and be successful are limited (we'll review them in the following point). Many brilliant product ideas by small Research Players have died before ever having the chance to consolidate, simply crushed by fierce competition coming from bigger and more powerful contenders. The ways they can do it are numerous and diverse, and most of them arise from either an exceedingly superior liquidity, a major channel dominance or unbearable customer acquisition costs.

The liquidity criteria can be used by the mass marketer or the Premium Player to launch a price war, defer payback or to increase required investments much beyond the Research Player capacity. Iberia, the largest Spanish airline, launched its low-cost subsidiary ClickAir in 2006 simply to crush its young and innovative competitor Vueling, which in just two years of existence had become an increasing threat to Iberia's dominance in the Spanish domestic market. By significantly lowering its prices (up to 54 percent on certain routes for example), and gladly embracing massive losses for its subsidiary as well, Iberia forced the Vueling-ClickAir merger in 2009. Once it was completed and the new company (which kept the Vueling brand, incidentally) started operating freely, its average prices surprisingly rocketed (an outstanding 68 percent on the route mentioned above) (Fageda, Jiménez and Perdiguero, 2010).

Channel dominance is normally used by the big company to prevent (or seriously hamper) the Research Player from gaining access to the distribution or supply network. Telefonica, for example, the fifth biggest broadband and telecommunications provider worldwide, has been frequently accused by its competitors of taking advantage of its practically total dominance over the network infrastructures to make competition as difficult as possible. If this is so for other big companies, imagine the competitive scenario for a Research Player with a promising innovation that requires a minimum bandwidth guaranteed or reasonable wholesale prices for network usage.

Finally, a captive market or massive brand exposure is used by mass marketers to increase acquisition costs and make it very difficult for Research Players to gain a decent market share. A recent example might be found in Near Field Communication (NFC), a payment method using mobile devices that has been experiencing some serious push lately when being adopted and boosted by some big mass marketers such as Google (Google Wallet), Master Card and Visa and many important banks worldwide. In contrast with this, start-ups like Flooz.com and Beenz (early 2000s), were absolutely unable to consolidate their proposed alternative online payment methods due to the lack of a credible backup (among other operating criteria).

3. Evolve into a Brand Leader

Of course, not all pictures are that gloomy. In some other scenarios, Research Players consolidate, grow and evolve into Brand Leaders.[5] The main difference between them (a Research Player and a Brand Leader) is caused by the different target scope, and lies in the fact that, as a company leveraged on Innovation grows and its value proposition becomes increasingly popular and cross-segmented, the sustainability of its cost structure forces it to progressively adopt an approach toward process standardization. This is very difficult to combine with Flexibility as another main competitive advantage, so that this is normally traded off against

---

5   Evolving into Brand Leaders is not unique to Research Players. As we will review in Section 4.4.7, Premium Players might also do it, but through a very different process and due to other reasons.

Service, starting a process that was described in Section 4.4.4. Furthermore, the rise of a new Brand Leader within a given business is a major disruption and typically comes along (or is caused by) a new dominant value paradigm.

For the evolution of a Research Player into a Brand Leader to happen, and in line with what has been explained in the previous point, it is necessary that bigger companies competing in the same (or somehow impacted) business allow its development and consolidation. This might happen either because they voluntarily allow it to do so (typically, due to an underestimation of its capacity to harm its value proposition) or because the swiftness of its growth and consolidation wrong-foots them. In either case, whenever the big players realize the actual threat to their value proposition, it is normally too late to react as described in point 2.

Typical examples of this situation might be found in the encyclopedia publishing business, successively turned upside down by disruptive innovations (both from the technologic and business point of view). Microsoft Encarta, a digital multimedia encyclopedia fairly popular from 1993 to late 2009, was eventually dismissed by the company due to its inability to adapt to the new value proposition posed by a back-then young Research Player, eventually destined to become a renowned Brand Leader, called Wikipedia. Encarta itself, in turn, had decisively contributed to the collapse of former business benchmark Encyclopedia Britannica, which had previously rejected its request to digitalize its contents.

Applied Example: WhatsApp

WhatsApp, however, stands as a paradigmatic example of a Research Player's sky-rocketing rise and evolution into a Brand Leader. As such, its competitive model is thus based on Innovation and Service. Indeed, the company's CEO, Jan Koum, announced at Mobile World Congress, 2014 in Barcelona the corporate's plans to include free voice calling as an addition to its cross-platform instant messaging services (Abboud and Auchard, 2014). This major innovation will definitely be changing the already turbulent telecommunication business, with sure implications for big, consolidated carriers. A business with 500 companies as monthly active users (Chart 4.9) handling 50 billion messages daily (Chart 4.10) is no longer a Research Player: it has such a massive value as a customer platform and such brand exposure worldwide that simply cannot be blocked by any other business player. The other carriers' value propositions will definitely have to evolve and strengthen, as happened for example when they were forced both to review their revenue streams (moving from voice calling to data transmission) and monetization model (widely launching flat-rate data plans for mobile and fixed Internet connection) as a result of the competition from Skype (the first global Voice-Over-Internet-Protocol (VOIP) provider) and its free long-distance calling.

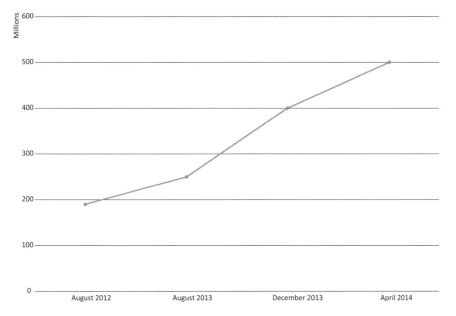

Chart 4.9   WhatsApp's number of monthly active users
Source: Data from Coldewey, 2014; WhatsApp, n.d.

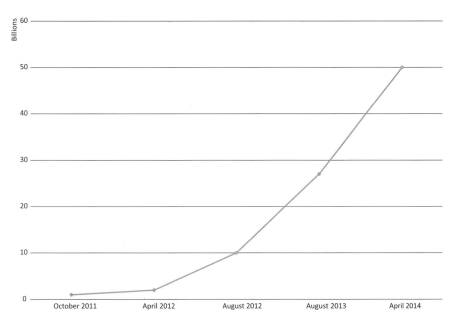

Chart 4.10   WhatsApp's number of daily messages
Source: Data from Coldewey. 2014; WhatsApp, n.d.

Some of the newborn Brand Leaders consolidate and endure through the years. Others, probably a majority, end up being acquired by even bigger players. Compared to what was envisioned during a company's earliest years as a Research Player, selling the company might look like a betrayal. But it is not: it is just business competition, and yet, after being acquired, these companies can still play a major role in their business by continuing to develop its value proposition even further.

At a conference in January, 2014, WhatsApp's CEO said (Coldewey, 2014): "It's not hard to sell a company, but if you look at companies today like Facebook, Google, Yahoo and Twitter, they didn't sell. They stuck around and built a great offering for users. For us it's about a company that is here to stay."

Barely one month later, WhatsApp was sold to Facebook for roughly $16 billion.

4.4.6 Lean Players

Carsharing is basically an evolution of rigid car rental services in which members rent cars for short periods of time (often by the hour) which can be found distributed anywhere around the service area (most frequently, located for access by public transport).

Applied Example: Zipcar

In 2000, two Massachusetts (US) residents founded Zipcar, a membership-based company for car drivers based on the carsharing core principle: to offer the benefits of private cars, without the costs and responsibilities of actually owning one. In 2013, the company was acquired by Avis Budget Group for roughly $500 million. Zipcar is an example of a Lean Player competitive model, based on a combination of Flexibility and Service.

As an all-included self-service, Zipcar members can book a car in any Zipcar city (spread through the US, Canada, UK, Spain and Austria) online (of course, mobile Apps are available) and have it immediately ready to use. Cars are unlocked through a member-exclusive access card containing a wireless chip that will only open it at the time it's been reserved. Driver's insurance and fuel costs are included in the rate: drivers find a gas card for refueling (alternatively, reimbursement is granted if the gas station does not accept it). Besides the aforementioned technology-based services, in 2009 Zipcar launched the FastFleet service to help public fleets managers optimize the operational costs and environmental benefits, while meeting their mobility needs.

Membership can be obtained through a "occasional driving plan," a pay-per-drive approach by which members have no monthly commitment (minimum number of hours booked) and just a reduced annual fee (around $50) or a "extra value plan," by which customers are granted discounts in hour fees in exchange for a minimum monthly use.

As mentioned in Section 4.4.2, niche players leverage their profitability (at least, from a long-term perspective) either on higher unitary margins or on segment exclusivity (large market shares within a given niche or customer segment). In the case of Zipcar, this is based on the latter. To begin with, and despite favorable growth forecasts, around 1.5 million carsharing members worldwide of an estimated total of 1.3 billion car owners (2013) represents a tiny 0.11 percent and, therefore, represents a niche market (probably linked to urban-based lifestyles). Chart 4.11 shows, however, that Zipcar accounts for a very significant share of this market (averaging an outstanding 41 percent market share for the period 2010–13).

From a value-offering analysis, the capacity to eliminate a heavy burden from its customers' day-to-day life and turn it into a service on demand stands as a very interesting example of how to apply the *Predation of Value* approach to reassess the process of driving from a product-based perspective (frequent driving justifies owning a car) to a customer-based one (users demand transportation, not a car) and eventually dismiss processes and agents involved that basically predate value (the ones involved in the car ownership).

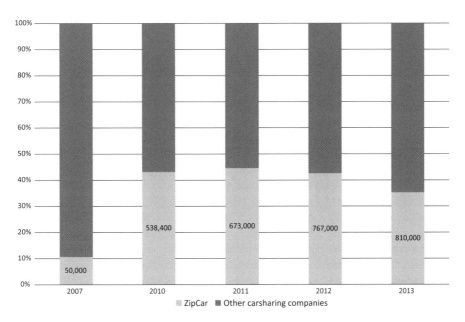

Chart 4.11   Zipcar Inc. market share (as a percentage of total carsharing members worldwide)

Source: Data from Navigant Research, 2013; Shaheen and Cohen 2012; Zipcar Reports 2010–12.

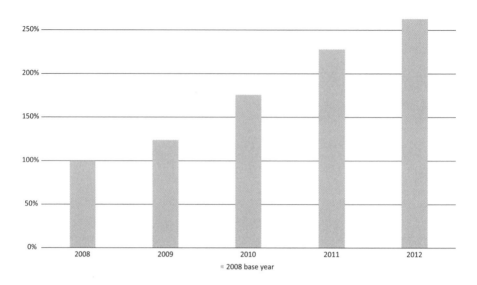

Chart 4.12   Zipcar Inc. revenue evolution
Source: Data from Zipcar n.d; Zipcar Reports 2010–12.

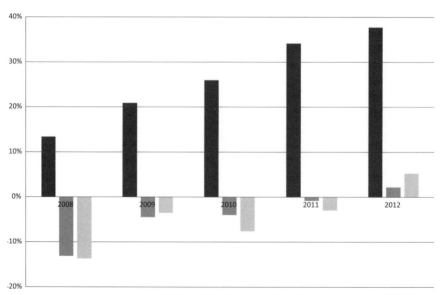

■ Gross margin ■ Operating margin ▪ Net margin

Chart 4.13   Key financial ratios for Zipcar Inc.
Source: Data from Zipcar n.d; Zipcar Reports 2010–12.

Flexibility, needless to say, is the core principle of Zipcar's value proposition and hence stated in its own tagline ("wheels when you want them"). Note how this competitive priority is reflected in every single aspect of Zipcar's business model, from the conceptualization of the value proposition (reduce car idle times, drive whenever you want) over the car location and availability, to the adaptable membership plans. Flexibility, as noted above, used as a way to eliminate a heavy burden. The problem is that the burden itself cannot be eliminated, but just transferred from the customer to the company. Cars still have to be purchased, financed, maintained and looked after—this means that if we want our customers to forget about these concerns and ensure on-demand use... we'll have to pay for it.

Thus, Flexibility for Lean Players is typically achieved at a high cost, and this is clearly reflected in their operating model and cost structure. This doesn't mean, of course, that this is, intrinsically, a non-profitable competitive model (we wouldn't be reviewing it, would we?) but rather requires either higher unitary margins or access to scale economies that, in a niche market, can only be achieved through a large segment dominance. Of course, this is a key issue to be addressed.

In the Zipcar example, despite an uninterrupted increase in its revenues (Chart 4.12) since 2008, its key financial figures indicate negative operating and net margins (Chart 4.13) from its very first fiscal year until 2012. In 2007, the company tried to address the low-volume issue by merging with Seattle-based Flexcar, thus creating a nationwide carsharing company. Although its financial results would still be negative for some further years, the company went public in 2011. The fact that a traditional car renting company purchased the company in 2013 suggests that future growth and more solid financial results are expected.

4.4.7 Premium Players

In *Competing on Eight Dimensions of Quality* (1987), David Garvin stated that *Quality* as a competitive positioning couldn't be restricted to a tangible, objective approach based on product reliability and process control, but should also contemplate other intangible dimensions reflecting a superior perceived value. Based on that, he posed an assessment model for Quality based on eight different dimensions.

From the TDV model approach, Garvin tried to encompass in a single definition the internal and external perspective of a brand attribute. As explained in Section 4.4 (and shown in Figure 4.4), the value proposition perspective primarily concerns the customer and is based on his/her brand perception *as a whole*. The competitive model perspective, however, is primarily related to the way the company creates this brand identity by structuring and consolidating an underlying competitive model that ensures its operating sustainability.

Thus, despite the consensus on the different nuances of the Quality concept when commonly used to refer to the value proposition of companies like Toyota and Ferrari, for example, from the internal perspective of the analysis the truth is that they do share some common approaches in terms of competitive priorities and operating focus. Indeed, Quality as an internal competitive priority is uniquely defined (Table 4.4), while Quality as a brand attribute is far more complex and linked to both aspirational and tangible attributes, not exclusively related to product features that are delivered by a combination of *Quality* itself and *Service*. Therefore, for a much more accurate use and to avoid misunderstandings, we shall refer to this attribute as *Premium* and hence the niche players delivering this value proposition as *Premium Players*.

The identity of the attribute Premium is built on the basis of three different dimensions (Figure 4.6), each one of them linked to a specific value delivery. This delivery is precisely made through a combination of Quality, Service (competitive priorities) and Price, which stands as a relevant factor as well (Table 4.6).

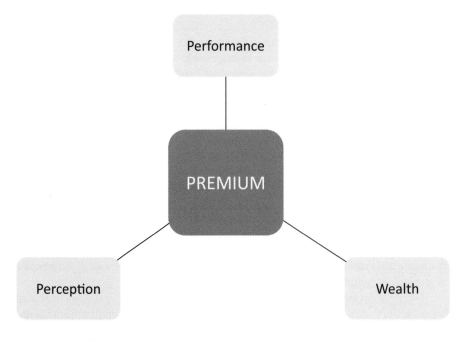

Figure 4.6   Dimensions of the attribute Premium

Table 4.6   Further dimensions of the attribute Premium

	Defined as	Related to	Delivered through		
			Quality	Service	Price
Performance	Functional Value	Durability, reliability, robustness	X		
Perception	Individual and Social Value	Prestige, self-identity, uniqueness		X	X
Wealth	Financial Value	Expensiveness, high residual value (products), scarcity	X	X	X

- The *Performance* dimension refers to any functional value delivered by the superior tangible features of a product or service, whether achieved through its components or manufacturing/deployment process. Thinking of a Ferrari car, for example, there are obvious tangible benefits coming from its outstanding specifications (engine performance, technology, materials and so on). This set of features endows it with superior durability, reliability or conformance to specifications among many other functionalities. The Performance dimension is mainly delivered through the Quality competitive priority.
- The *Perception* dimension refers to any intangible individual and social value perceived by the customer, such as prestige, self-identity enhancement or uniqueness. As a purely subjective dimension, it is composed by a combination of different factors deeply related with an experiential and relational perspective (as developed in Section 3.2.1 when speaking of the Appreciation dimension of value) merging to create a specific brand background for the customer. In the Ferrari example, and going beyond the fact that the car is *really* offering a superior performance, it would not have the Premium condition unless agreed upon by a vast majority of the market and therefore perceived as such. The Brand itself plays a key role in achieving this (you may want to review the Automotive Business Applied Example in Chapter 3, and more specifically the point in which the different value perceived in two identical BMW cars, but one of them without any brand symbol, is discussed) although how to actually do it exceeds the scope of this book. Precisely due to this intangible, aspirational approach, we may conclude that the Perception dimension is delivered through the Service competitive priority and Price (as an attribute).
- The *Wealth* dimension refers to the financial value of the good in the market, and thus it is related to its higher unitary price, scarcity and forecasted residual value (only when speaking of products, there's no residual value for services). To put it in other words: something expensive and rare is perceived as valuable and, therefore, likely to maintain its value (or even

increase it) over the long term. Both expensive services and products, however, require a coherent justification to legitimate its higher price, and this is mainly related to tangible attributes. Just as a cheap Ferrari car would immediately raise suspicion, a normally priced one with poorer (note that the word is *poorer* and not *poor*) materials, components or performance would rapidly see its market value decreased. The Wealth dimension is delivered by the Quality and Service competitive priorities and the Price attribute.

Premium Players are therefore niche players offering a Premium value proposition that, from the internal perspective, is delivered through a competitive model based on Quality and Service. As above mentioned, brand identity and its condition of aspirational brand is a key success factor, and this is why Premium Players are normally global. Some examples of Premium Players, besides the aforementioned Ferrari, might be Prada, Lego or The Boston Consulting Group (specialized management consulting services).

Applied Example: Prada Inc.

In a much more acute way than other niche players, Premium Players base their financial and operating sustainability on higher unitary margins, most typically traded off against high volumes. As depicted in the comparison of key financial metrics for some contenders of the fashion-retail business (Chart 4.4), for instance, the Italian retailer Prada is clearly above all other companies shown in the example either from the gross margin and the operating margin perspective (profit ratios, however, are fluctuant as influenced by financial criteria). Let's consider the gross margin ratio, for example: this is the difference between the revenue coming from the goods sold, less the cost of the material used to manufacture (and the manufacturing cost itself) as a percentage of total sales. The fact that this ratio is, on average, 157 percent higher than Gap's for the 2011–13 period (Chart 4.14) simply means than Prada is much better than Gap at convincing its customers of its superior added value (the same applies, to a lesser extent, for Inditex). If we try to analyze it from the Premium attribute point of view described above, this might come from either the Performance (functional dimension) of its products (better fabrics, enhanced durability and so on), the customer perception of prestige or the financial value of the product by itself. The truth is that, like almost any other firm in the business, Prada outsources a huge percentage of its production to low-cost countries like China, Vietnam, Turkey and Romania, hence eliminating the "crafted at home" factor that possibly contributed to its reputation in its early days. Despite the fact that the fabrics used might very well be of a better quality, it certainly seems that this is not the most important reason on which Prada leverages its better result. If we focus on the operating margin instead, thus including all costs of sales (fixed costs as well), and contrary to what might be assumed because of Prada having to face the cost of better services, Chart 4.14 shows that the differences versus competitors have become even greater!

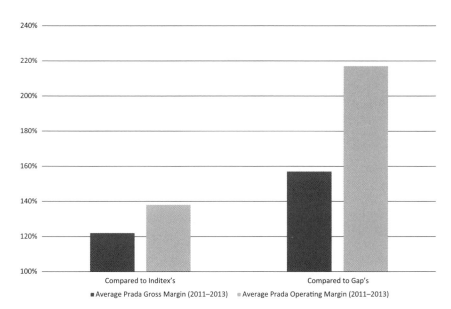

Chart 4.14   A comparison of Prada's key financial ratios
Source: Data from Bloomberg Businessweek, 2014a, b, c.

Again, this superior added value is, by no means, exclusively linked to tangible benefits, but also to a higher perception of the Premium attribute which, in turn, is primarily linked to the Brand experience (of course, this is largely leveraged on Quality and Service) and reflected in its selling price.

All in all, and considering this, a key success factor for Premium Players is the selection of the right market niche in which to deliver a value proposition built upon Quality and Service that might be appreciated. And what is a right market niche? Well, one that combines a high purchasing power of its members with a significant global size.

4.5 KEY TAKEAWAYS

- The internal analysis deals with the creation of value within the company. The essential requirement for a value position to be successful is to be easily identifiable and clearly different from others.
- A company uses its internal levers for value generation to achieve the corporate goals and progressively position in the market according to an identifiable competitive model.
- The corporate goals must be defined according to the SMART methodology: specific, measurable, assignable, relevant and time-framed.

- There are three types of corporate goals, each one of them directly linked to one of the Three Dimensions of Value: Waiter Goals (Appreciation), Cook Goals (Concentration) and Sweeper Goals (Predation).
- The internal levers are the different fields and associate resources a company might work with to generate value and serve its global strategy. There are three different levers within a company: Structure, Specialization and Process Management. Each lever has different *focuses*.
- The *Structure* lever deals with anything related with the organizational design, corporate architecture, talent recruitment and staff empowerment. It encompasses the People and Organization focuses.
- The *Specialization* lever concerns about the generation of a cross-company level of both strategic and operating excellence and know-how. It encompasses the Expertise and Positioning focuses.
- The *Process Management* lever is concerned with every activity related to the conceptualization, planning, monitoring and execution of long-term corporate focus, scope and processes. It encompasses the Harvesting and Exploring focuses.
- The competitive model is the translation of the value proposition from the perspective of the company.
- The company's competitive model is composed of a combination of competitive priorities.
- There are five competitive priorities: Cost, Quality, Service, Innovation and Flexibility.
- The number of competitive models is theoretically unlimited, but the reality is that successful companies tend to use very consolidated and identifiable models.
- Successful mass marketers tend to be either Efficiency Leaders (a combination of Quality, Cost and Flexibility) or Brand Leaders (a combination of Innovation and Service).
- Successful niche players tend to be either Research Players (a combination of Innovation and Flexibility), Lean Players (a combination of Service and Flexibility) or Premium Players (a combination of Quality and Service).

CHAPTER 5

MEASURING AND CONTROLLING YOUR RESULTS

5.1 APPROACH

The well-known foundations of Project Management establish five main phases to successfully approach any of them.[1] Of these, the essential core is composed by three types of activities: *Planning, Execution* and *Monitoring*. As we move from the former to the latter, we progressively abandon the theoretical perspective to get into the real-life one, and this typically means contingencies and unforeseen difficulties to be faced. Indeed, whenever having a solid strategic planning is absolutely mandatory to achieve success in any business endeavor (review Chapter 1 again if you are thinking of the importance of intuition at this point), knowing and understanding the results of said strategy is what makes the difference in terms of the real competitiveness of our value proposition. That said, the truth is that most managers (project, account or top manager, the hierarchy level doesn't really matter), when looking back, report a shortfall in resources devoted to the last two stages aforementioned, and especially Monitoring. The reasons for this are manifold:

1. Monitoring is less rewarding

Monitoring involves controlling, and more precisely controlling processes, resources, behaviors… and people. The problem is that is difficult to delimit some processes, quantify resources and observe behaviors—people don't usually like to be controlled.

Let's face it: for most people, creating something from scratch is far more fun or creative than actually controlling its outcomes. This typically requires a process-driven, standardized approach frequently linked to business intelligence, data mining and reporting activities, frequently considered less appealing. However, this can be solved by assigning the right professional profiles to these types of jobs, on one hand, and striving to enhance visibility on the underlying business

---

1   Initiate, Plan, Execute, Monitor and Control, Close.

approach, on the other. Indeed, many professionals have a data-driven profile and, consequently, feel comfortable handling these types of procedures. In addition, if we ensure their understanding of how these processes fit within the corporate global strategy, the overall performance will surely be improved. Note that, from this point of view, it is normally a bad idea to assign the same people that have been deeply involved in the strategy definition to monitor its results. First and foremost, because of the so-called *interviewer bias* (a partiality toward a preconceived, desired response or process outcome whether or not conscious), but also because these two activities typically require different skills (analytic–synthetic with a global vision as the first profile, and detail-driven and thoughtful as the second one). This by no means implies that strategists should not have any contact with the monitoring and controlling phase (in fact, it is imperative, basically because strategists are normally top managers as well), but instead should not be involved in the reporting of the *results* (not process).

2. Monitoring demands further action

As noted above, thinking is mandatory but turning things into reality is what really makes the difference. Entrepreneurs know this very well, as typically there's a significant gap between their initial business plan and what they finally do. This shouldn't demerit strategic planning, but just reinforce the idea that the sequence depicted in Figure 2.2 about how to approach a business the right way, is, in fact, not a linear sequence but a circular one in which the results of the monitoring phase serves as a critical feedback to further adapt and modify strategy. If we divest monitoring of this circular dimension and consider it the ultimate stage, an end in itself, then it becomes senseless. In other words: the outcomes of the monitoring phase demand further action to be taken, and this is somehow pushy. Let's review an example to further clarify it.

Assume that the strategic assessment of a company concludes that some internal processes should be optimized to help contain operating costs. Among many other initiatives included in a comprehensive document, that requires an optimization and control of working hours and working times to enhance productivity. Then the Execution stage begins: it is time to start deploying what is contained in the strategic guidelines, and hence time attendance devices are installed in the manufacturing plants. Although initially planned exclusively for plant workers, this creates a sense of discrimination when compared to other company divisions, and eventually leads to the installation of said devices everywhere. This Monitoring process generates a huge amount of information which unexpectedly reveals a significant and general discrepancy between planned and real working times ... concerning office workers. Of course, this category includes low-level employees, but also middle and senior managers. This is, needless to say, important information for top managers, but absolutely useless unless they actually take some kind of decision based on it (such as disciplinary measures, employee relocation underpinned by absenteeism ratios of different divisions and so on). However, after testing the waters with some heads of department, and given their reluctance to adopt such unpopular measures, these actions are finally dismissed: after all, the initial actions were aimed at plant workers and not at office employees (whose schedule is naturally harder to be tracked), right?

In this example, the outcome of the monitoring phase demands actions, both from the perspective of redefining internal procedures (recruiting, employee control and task assignation, and so on) and, potentially, the critical reassessment of corporate culture. This information, undoubtedly, could constitute a meaningful feedback to adjust the strategic planning of the company, but is ultimately dismissed simply because the top management line is unable to push ahead. The overall conclusion is that monitoring is useless, time-consuming and aggressive. This is a frequent scenario, which wrongly leads to further belittling the importance of monitoring when it should be regretting the inappropriateness (or absence) of the actions taken instead.

3. Monitoring involves confronting harsh reality

Planning is always easier than dealing with real-life situations and taking hard decisions. Confronting reality sometimes involves assuming that what we initially planned turned out to be either wrong, inaccurate or useless. That means frustration and, most definitely, additional work. Most people don't like that, so they undermine the importance of monitoring and control the results, typically by saying that either certain things cannot be measured or they are not worth the effort.

Concerning the former, it is important to note everything can be measured either from the point of view of the actions in themselves or their tangible effects. Add to this the limitless opportunities that the combination of digital technologies and statistic offer nowadays and you'll conclude that the first statement is largely false.

Regarding the latter, this is typically linked to the overestimation of intuition-based scenarios (again, you may want to review Chapter 1). Even if we neglect that this might very well jeopardize the deployment of the strategy, we should consider that although launching an integrated model of monitoring (for a specific aspect or at a general level) might entail some initial start-up costs, they tend to decrease over time and soon be outweighed by their benefits. Think about the decision-making process of a surgeon during an open-heart surgery, and assume that you are the patient on the operation table: would you like it to be 100 percent intuition-based, or would you rather prefer that the hospital has invested in the latest available technology, even if expensive? Clear enough, right? Well, you should follow the same principle regarding business management: it is (almost) as critical.

4. Monitoring is normally seen under an internal customer approach

Unfortunately, this is not so much a misconception but the result of a frequent misapplication of the core concepts of strategic analysis. Indeed, as explained throughout Chapter 2, the core benchmark to assess the results of the strategy deployment should be found in the competitive environment (business) and not inside the company. This doesn't mean that internal performance indicators should not be considered, but simply that all of them should serve a higher purpose: contributing to increase the company competitiveness and the value of its most valuable assets: the market assets. These are essential measures of the company's long-term value under a demand perspective. We will be reviewing in depth the key aspects of market asset valuation and other metrics of competitiveness in the following sections, as this is a key aspect of the chapter. For the moment, let's just say that monitoring the corporate performance is a two-way street between the company and the business in which it competes. A common mistake, especially in big corporations, is somehow losing contact with the outside world (business) to focus on the internal one, and that is when the staff start thinking that they work for their respective bosses (internal customer), instead of for the final customer. Coming back to the surgery example, this would be the equivalent of defining a comprehensive list of procedures and indicators to monitor if the surgery equipment is in good condition or the surgical team arrives on time while paying no attention to whether the patient is still alive or not.

While reviewing the key requirements of a successful business approach in Chapter 1, we emphasized the necessity of considering practice over talent. Remember what was pointed out in Section 4.4 regarding the competitive model versus the value proposition dilemma: despite all clichés regarding unplanned and immediate lucky strikes in business, success is an iterative process. Thus, monitoring and controlling the results of the strategy stands as the core, though frequently understated process, within the global approach to a successful competition. In Figure 2.2, we summarized our final goal through a question included in process 6: "P&L bottom line: how can I improve it?" and mentioned how this essential metric set out the deep interrelation between internal and external perspectives. At this point, hopefully, this is much more clarified, although to fully grasp it we still need to build a model to integrate both points of view. Before we do that, however, we shall go deeper into the market assets concept and how to measure them.

5.1.1 Market Assets Valuation

First and foremost, a disclaimer: this is the only section of this book in which you can expect a certain (small) amount of mathematics and financial ratios. For those readers simply unable to bear math, our sincere apologies and the promise of a straightforward approach. After all, five or six formulas are the least that could have been expected of a chapter about performance indicators!

But let us get to the point. Differently than any other corporate assets (such as buildings, receivables or patents) and despite their key importance, the measuring and assessment of market assets have been largely ignored from the managerial point of view until recently, maybe because of their intangible nature and their difficult quantification. As noted above, market assets stand as measures of the company's long-term value under a demand perspective and therefore a cornerstone of any performance assessment procedure. Precisely in its long-range and inclusive approach is where its main added value might be found: counterbalancing short-term bias typically induced by traditional metrics included in corporate decision-support systems (mainly, P&L figures and ratios) that focus almost exclusively on the immediate results achieved.

The conceptualization of markets assets has been a recurring matter of study among practitioners (of course, it's not our goal to deliver a comprehensive analysis on this topic but focus on its operational translation). Traditionally, there has been a general consensus around the desirability of using two different approaches that has lately led to the consolidation of two main metrics.

Brand Equity
The first approach concerns what the company is offering to the market and consequently constitutes its main sign of identity: the brand. The metric emanating from this concept is called *Brand Equity*. For those readers requiring an academic definition of this concept, this might a good moment to bring up what one of the main researchers on the topic once stated (Winters, 1991): "if you ask ten people to define Brand Equity, you are likely to get ten (maybe 11) different answers as to what it means." This said, the best one (perhaps because of its soundness), might be "the annualized incremental contribution of the brand in regards of the basic product or service" (Srinivasan and Hanssens, 2009).

Be that as it may, the first thing to learn about Brand Equity is that no single metric can be used to conceptualize and measure it, as it encompass a heterogeneous set of benefits that must be tracked separately. Table 5.1 gathers a proposal of the ten most salient metrics to be tracked in order to get an accurate picture, in what might be called the Brand Equity Statement. Of these, the first nine metrics are based on a well-known a consolidated model (Aaker, 1996), whereas the last one represents the quantitative, financial-based perspective of Brand Valuation which is the main research contribution on this matter for these last years. Therefore, the metrics included in the Brand Equity Statement deal with key aspects within the brand–market relationship, such as customer perception in regards of a specific attribute, preference over competitors or said financial value of the brand.

It is important to note that, by their nature, these metrics are either quantitative or qualitative, and hence cannot be summarized in a single measure. The best way of measuring qualitative metrics is by using a so-called Likert-type scale, the most widely used approach to scaling responses in survey research by which respondents specify their level of agreement or disagreement for a series of statements. The full range of the scale varies, typically fluctuating between 1 (strongly disagree) and 5 (strongly agree).

The measurement methodology for Brand Valuation, in turn, changes from case to case. Interbrand's model, for example, removes estimated earnings coming from tangible assets from total earnings (Rocha, n.d.). Among many other examples, a very practical methodology (see Figure 5.1) to approach Brand Equity valuation assigns an economic value to the brand based on different market-based metrics, hence allowing further comparison that constitutes a very graphic benchmark for assessment (Farris et al., 2006).

On a final note, and from the point of view of managerial implications, a key aspect to highlight is that the validity and utility of the model is leveraged on two main criteria:

1. a time-sustained and standardized data-gathering process;
2. a comparative assessment (on fiscal year or period basis) of the attained results.

Every company, therefore, should customize a specific Brand Equity Statement that proves useful, reasonably practicable and adapted to its competitive model. More than any particular metric included in the model, what really makes a difference is its careful implementation.

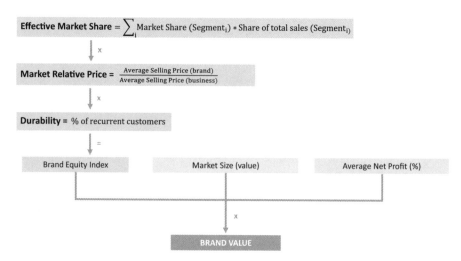

Figure 5.1   A Brand Valuation model
Source: Author's diagram, based on Farris et al., 2006.

Table 5.1   Brand Equity Statement: different metrics

Metric	Definition	Suggested measure
Satisfaction	Direct measure of customer satisfaction within a certain timeframe	Likert-type scale
Price Premium	Additional amount a customer would pay for the brand in comparison with another (benchmark)	Percentage
Perceived Quality	Degree to which the quality of the brand (not the product) is perceived to be better than a set of benchmarks	Likert-type scale
Leadership	Degree to which the brand is recognized as innovative and providing advances in product or service	Likert-type scale
Perceived Value	Whether the brand provides good value for the money or reasons to buy it over competitors	Likert-type scale
Brand Personality	Brand-as-a-person perspective. Links to the emotional perspective or self-expressive benefits of the brand	Likert-type scale, based on attributes
Organizational Associations	Brand-as-an-organization perspective, degree of affinity with corporate values	Liket-type scale, based on statements
Awareness	Salience of the brand in the customer's mind (recognition, recall, top-of-mind)	Yes/No, Inclusion in recall list
Market Price and Distribution Coverage	Average Selling Price (Brand) divided by Average Selling Price (Business), number of stores carrying the brand	Percentage
Brand Valuation	Financial-based forecast of brand value from a comparative perspective	Various*

*   The methodology differs from case to case.

Customer Equity

The second approach concerns who is being targeted with the company's value proposition, and therefore constitutes its basic benchmark for future sustainability: the customer. The metric that reflects the economic value of the entire customer body is called *Customer Equity*.

The importance of Customer Equity as a metric lies in its ability to reflect future earnings. However, as happens with Brand Equity, its real added value must be understood in the context of an integrated perspective that enables a cause-and-effect assessment.

Differently from Brand Equity, which encompasses a heterogeneous set of different quantitative and qualitative measures, Customer Equity is a purely quantitative, single metric that reflects the economic value of the entire customer basis. Research in that field has been, again, significant during these past few years, resulting in the consolidation of a measurement paradigm based on cash flow forecast. Based on it, the so-called Customer Lifetime Value (CLV) is defined as *the present value of the projected future cash flows from the customer relationship* (Gupta et al., 2006), or, in other words, the discounted benefit coming from a customer throughout his/her entire relationship with the company. There are different models to calculate CLV (including some of indisputable complexity, such as those based on RFM[2] models or others based on probabilistic models). Among them, a fairly simple and common, yet solid one (Farris et al., 2006), establishes a methodology based on just two variables (the discount rate, the third used metric, is defined as the interest rate to discount future events in a multi-period model, and might be established by each company):

1. Customer margin: Defined as the difference between revenues coming from a customer and the costs involved in the customer relationship. Of course, this metric requires a solid assignment procedure for both revenues and costs that becomes much easier to have in the case of contractual relationships. This said, and in response to the objection of the difficulty to precisely calculate them, this might be a good time to emphasize the need for an estimate of both customer revenue and customer costs, independently of the interest in developing a market asset valuation procedure. This applies to any given company competing in whatever business, so that if the methodology presented here simply does not fit a specific company, we strongly encourage the development of a customized methodology to do so.
2. The retention rate of customers: defined as the number of customers retained as a percentage of the total, therefore a loyalty measure. The complement of this rate is called customer churn (a very popular measure within subscription-based businesses).
3. Based on them, the CLV might be calculated as:

$$CLV = \frac{\text{Retention Rate}(\%)}{1 + \text{Discount Rate}(\%) - \text{Retention Rate}(\%)} \times \text{Customer Margin}$$

Where

$$\text{Customer Margin} = \text{Customer Revenues} - \text{Customer Costs}$$

---

2   *Recency, Frequency, Monetary Value.* These type of models pose a characterization of customer groups based on these three variables, as they have proved their accuracy as predictors for customer behavior.

And hence Customer Equity might be considered the sum of all CLV for the entire company's customer basis:

$$\text{Customer Equity} = \sum_i \text{CLV}_i$$

Brand Equity and Customer Equity will stand as key pillars of our future integrated model to monitor the corporate performance. A model that shall encompass both an internal and external perspective of the value generated by the company in different timeframes.

5.2 THE CREATION OF AN INTEGRATED MODEL

As mentioned in Section 5.1, and in line with the so-called *optimized way of approaching business* (Figure 2.2), and integrated assessment model of the corporate performance should combine an internal and an external perspective. Likewise external analysis, and therefore the proper understanding of the implications of the Three Dimensions of Value (TDV) within a given business (Figure 3.10), preceded the definition of corporate goals, the identification of internal actions to achieve them and the progressive consolidation of a recognizable competitive model (Figure 4.1). The process of monitoring the overall performance of our strategic plan cannot be limited to the evaluation of the extent of targets compliance and the efficient deployment of the available levers for value generation. By doing so, we would be rather focusing on the *effectiveness* of our plan (optimization of resources) instead of on its *efficiency* (its contribution to the corporate goals).

Indeed, as reviewed in Section 5.1.1, this is a common misapplication of the strategy deployment and monitoring process. We shall call it the *reviewer myopia*. To understand what it is about, let's get back to the applied example of Sparkatronics in Chapter 4.

If you remember, we left our friends from the car repair shop in the middle of a major restructuring process resulting from a thorough application of the TDV model and the subsequent identification of new corporate goals based on the waiter–cook–sweeper structure (Table 4.1). These goals further led to the definition of a comprehensive package of actions based on the use of the three internal levers (Structure, Specialization, Process Management) and their respective focus (Table 4.3).

Let's assume that the process of strategy deployment has moved on, and now it's time to assess its overall performance. Take a sample goal within the list and some of its related actions:

- B3 (a cook goal): Reduce average selling price (ASP) by 15 percent per customer within two fiscal years. Actions taken (not comprehensive):
  - Based on the Specialization Lever–Expertise Focus: Create a detailed cost-evaluation process for each type of car categories.
  - Based on the Process Management Lever–Harvesting Focus: Evaluate supplier policy to push down average acquisition costs.

The standard monitoring process would typically include a two-step review. In the first step, the degree of compliance of the actions would be assessed on the basis of the different levels of performance indicators established (we'll review the definition of indicators in Section 5.2.3). The reviewer would verify, for example, the number of car categories that had gone through a cost-evaluation process and compare this number with the indicator previously set. Something similar would happen with action 2: the reviewer would compare the new purchasing costs with the previous ones and see whether they had decreased or not.

The second step would include an assessment of the new ASP to check its pace of reduction (and, again, compare it with a previously defined control indicator).

Imagine now that all mentioned actions had been completed with a satisfactory degree of compliance with the initial objectives: the number of car categories for which the cost-evaluation process had been done would be high enough and the purchasing costs had been indeed pushed down. The ASP, besides, had been reduced by 8 percent at the end of the first fiscal year and, consequently, the company would be more than half the way there in just one year. Given this situation, the theory of the *reviewer myopia* tells us that the reviewer himself would be very satisfied and, therefore, would conclude that the strategy deployment had been a complete success. But, would he be right? The answer is unknown: no clear conclusions can be drawn in the absence of additional reviews.

Indeed, the reviewer is just half the way there. For the result assessment process to be completed, the monitoring procedure must also contemplate how these actions have enhanced the company's competitiveness from a business perspective. If they haven't the degree of compliance or optimized resource consumption, it doesn't really matter, because the problem is the same as before: they are useless (if not harmful).

For example, it might very well be possible that, despite the fact that Sparkatronics' ASP has decreased by 8 percent, this is actually doing no good to the company, because it causes a misperception of lower quality and, consequently, a decrease in Brand Equity.

In fact, what we are checking through this business-level verification is the actual alignment of the corporate goals that have been defined with the global competitive position of the company. That is to say, the causal relationship between them. In the example above, the internal processes that led to an overall reduction of the company's ASP don't need a revision. What really needs to be rethought is whether this goal is actually strengthening the company's value proposition.

Does this mean that the degree of compliance with the objectives of the internal actions should not be monitored? Certainly not. It means that it's simply not enough. In Section 5.1, we defined the monitoring procedure as a two-way street between the company and the business in which it competes, and therefore we can conclude that our integrated model of monitoring (Figure 5.2) requires two different types of metrics entailing two different perspectives: we shall call them *inside-out* and *outside-in* metrics.

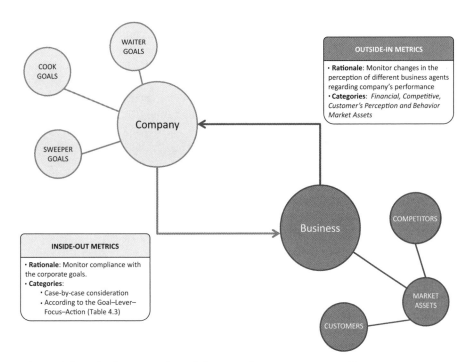

Figure 5.2   An integrated model to monitor corporate performance

5.2.1 Outside-in Metrics

The outside-in (OI, hereafter) type of metrics monitor changes in the perception of different business agents regarding company's performance (note how this incorporates a company-as-a-person overtone). As such, these perceptual changes cause further fluctuations in the value of the company's market assets. OI metrics have, therefore, a business-to-company direction of flow (hence its name) and serve as essential benchmarks to understand the real added value of the actions taken to achieve the corporate goals (or, as mentioned in the last section, to focus on their effectiveness and not only on their efficiency).

From a conceptual point of view, OI metrics may concern different business agents, and therefore be customer-focused or competitor-focused. Under this perspective, they are divided up into four main categories: *financial* (concerning P&L statements under a quantitative approach), *competitive* (concerning the interaction with other competitors within the business), *customer's perception and behavior* and *market assets*.

Table 5.2 gathers a set of suggested OI metrics, together with their calculation approach and an interpretation of their meaning (you'll notice how some of them have been interpreted accordingly in several applied examples throughout the different chapters). However, it is important to emphasize that this a proposal: as mentioned in past sections within this chapter, the capacity to measure corporate performance and correctly grasp the competitiveness of the company's value proposition lies in the degree of customization of the chosen metrics. Although the approach is deliberately generic, some of them might be considered useless or too hard to calculate for a specific company. If so, we encourage the reader to substitute them with other more useful ones.

Table 5.2   Outside-in metrics and their added value

Category	Suggested Metrics	Description	Added Value information
Financial	Sales	• Sales revenue	• Attractiveness of value proposition (customer perspective)
	Gross Margin	• Total revenues less cost of goods sold, calculated as a percentage of total revenues	• Manufacturing and purchasing efficiency
	Operating Margin	• Total revenues less operating expenses (including selling and general expenses), as a percentage of total revenues	• Global efficiency of the operating model

Category	Suggested Metrics	Description	Added Value information
Financial	Net Profit	• Total revenues less total costs, as a percentage of total. Also called "bottom line"	• Sustainability of the competitive model
	Market size Evolution	• Total sales (volume, revenues) in the market for year t as a percentage of its value for year (t-1)	• Market attractiveness (company perspective)
Competitive	Revenue Market Share	• Sales revenue as a percentage of total market sales revenue	• Comparative attractiveness of the value proposition (customer perspective)
	Relative Price	• Revenue market share divided by Unit Market Share	• Price-based company's positioning
	Market Penetration	• Number of purchasers as a percentage of total population	• For mass marketers: value proposition awareness (customer perspective) • For niche players: assessment of market niche size
Customer's Perception and Behavior	Loyalty	• Percentage of clients declaring repurchasing intention	• Degree of consolidation of the value proposition (customer perspective)
	Average Revenue per Customer	• (if available) Total sales revenue divided by total number of customers	• Understanding of the competitive model (Margin versus Turnover perspective)
	Customer Acquisition Costs	• Customer acquisition expenditures as a percentage of sales revenue	• Transactional link: characterization of industry rivalry (company perspective) • Relational link: degree of attractiveness of the experience included in the value proposition (customer perspective)
Market Assets	Brand Equity	• Brand Equity Statement (see Section 5.1)	• See Section 5.1.1
	Customer Equity	• Customer Equity	• See Section 5.1.1

5.2.2 Inside-out Metrics

Inside-out (IO hereafter) metrics monitor compliance with the corporate goals and, more specifically, the actions taken under each internal lever (remember: Structure, Process Management and Specialization) and their respective focus (you may want to review Section 4.3 and Figure 4.3). IO metrics have a company-to-business direction of flow in the sense that the actions to be measured are generated from within the company and ultimately they impact its competitive environment (business).

Differently from OI metrics, IO ones are not fixed, but vary based on the specific actions defined to achieve the different goals. The measurement process, therefore, is customized and would typically be based on the two-step approach explained in Section 5.2.

In the Sparkatronics case, for example, the action *Create a detailed cost-evaluation process for each type of car categories* could lead to the definition of two metrics:

1. number of car categories for which a detailed cost report has been issued;
2. percentage of shops adopting the new cost-assignment process.

The first step would determine whether the objectives for this action had been met, whereas the second step would check if the objectives for the corporate goal (reduce ASP by 15 percent in two fiscal years) under which the actions were defined had been equally met.

Finally, the level of achievement of these and every other OI and IO metric is determined on the basis of a predefined benchmark: the key performance indicators (KPIs).

5.2.3 Defining Key Performance Indicators

KPIs define a set of values that are designed to be measured against. They represent the reference value for the set of both IO and OI metrics, and therefore, an objective way to gauge their performance.

A proper definition of KPIs is aligned with the SMART (see Section 4.2) approach to defining corporate goals (in fact, it is nothing but its logical follow-up), and therefore are based on the assumption that they are specific, measurable, assignable, realistic and time-framed.

On the other hand, just as happens with test scores, the assessment outcome is rarely an OK/NOK or any other binary response. Of course, failing or passing as exam is the ultimate indicator of performance, but, once this is known, a comprehensive assessment should include other considerations, such as, for example, how close we have been to passing it (is not the same as scoring 10 points out of 100, which would indicate a significant lame performance, rather than scoring 45 out of 100, which would indicate that we are close to a minimally acceptable performance). On the other hand, our level of ambition in regards to the expected result will also condition our degree of satisfaction with the obtained score. Should we have worked hard for the exam and therefore we expect a very good score, getting 75 or 80 points out of 100 might disappoint us. Each case is different!

In conclusion, we can contemplate two criteria to define the KPIs:

1. A first one, to gauge how aggressively we want to pursue the objective. This criteria defines a multi-scenario approach, each one more demanding than the previous scenario:
   a. Aggressive: the most demanding scenario. Caution: make sure that this level is achievable, otherwise you'd be wasting your resources.
   b. Loose: the less demanding scenario. Caution: make sure that this level grants a sufficient level of compliance with the objectives, otherwise it would be useless.
   c. Neutral: the moderate scenario. Caution: may not necessarily correspond to a 50 percent degree of compliance.
2. One to help us *modulate the degree of satisfaction with the results obtained*, typically by using a multi-level scale that enables an assessment flexible enough. The most traditional way to do this is by using a three-level indicator system based on colors (because of its intuitive approach). The degree of compliance with the objectives that correspond to each one of them may vary from case to case, but must be previously defined anyway.
   a. Red: to indicate a poor performance and a subsequent urge to review the assessed process.
   b. Yellow: to raise a warning about the results obtained, typically on the edge of being considered unacceptable.
   c. Green: to indicate full compliance with the objectives.

Finally, the combination of these two criteria would result in a KPI Matrix. Assume, for example, that the metric to be controlled is *Number of monthly customer complaints*. The KPI Matrix based on which we could base our assessment could be something like that:

This type of structure should be replicated for every single metric, either IO or OI. Remember: the more customized the set of metric is and the more accurate and realistic their objectives are, the clearer the picture of our competitive performance from both an effectiveness and efficacy perspective would be.

Table 5.3   The Key Performance Indicator Matrix

	Green	Yellow	Red
Aggressive	0	Between 1 and 3	More than 3
Neutral	Less than 2	Between 2 and 5	More than 5
Loose	Less than 5	Between 5 and 10	More than 10

5.3 KEY TAKEAWAYS

- The successful definition and implementation of our strategy requires a sustained process of feedback.
- An essential benchmark to assess corporate performance is the fluctuation of value of the market assets. There are two main type of market assets: Brand Equity and Customer Equity.
- Brand Equity represents the annualized incremental contribution of the brand in regards to the basic product or service. Its definition requires a multidimensional approach, gathered in a set of ten metrics called the Brand Equity Statement.
- Customer Equity reflects the economic value of the entire customer body. It is defined as the sum of all CLVs.
- The CLV is defined as the present value of the projected future cash flows from the customer relationship.
- Monitoring the results achieved involves assessing them from both an effectiveness (do the right things) and efficiency (do the things right) perspective.
- An integrated model of monitoring involves either business-to-company (outside-in metrics) and company-to-business (inside-out metrics)
- Outside-in metrics monitor changes in the perception of different business agents regarding company's performance. They are divided into four main categories: financial, competitive, customer's perception and behavior, market assets.
- Inside-out metrics monitor compliance with corporate goals. They are defined according to the Goal–Lever–Focus–Action structure and calculated based on a case-by-case consideration.
- The level of achievement of every metric is assessed on the basis of KPIs.
- KPIs define a set of values that are used to measure against. To establish them, two different criteria are used: how aggressively we want to pursue the objective, on one hand, and the degree of satisfaction with the results obtained.
- These criteria are combined to create the KPI Matrix that must be established for every metric prior to the beginning of the monitoring process.

EPILOGUE

So, we finally made it to the end of the process. We have embraced the principles of value-based competitive analysis and defined a solid competitive model based on the thorough observation of the business dynamics and the creation of a differential value proposition. Along the way, we've always kept our customers at the very center of our strategy, developing a time-sustained process to be close to them and understand their insights. Besides, we've aligned our internal corporate resources around this winning strategy. We've wrapped our products and services with an outstanding experience, or rather decided to create an undisputed cost-cutting operating model that can beat every competitor in the market battleground. Finally, we've developed an accurate methodology to help us track our progresses and fine tune our actions.

We've made it. It's a beautiful day. So, what's next?

Well, start over. Again and again, as many times as required, breaking your own conventional wisdom all over again. Remember: successful competition is not a linear process, with a beginning and an end, but a permanently ongoing endeavor. Review all the examples presented along the book and you will see many once-successful business stories that eventually came to an end. Sometimes this is inevitable, but many others are essentially the result of complacency. Reinventing ourselves might be hard, but it is definitely rewarding. After all, it's all about being on the trail: the value trail.

REFERENCES

Aaker, D., 1996. Measuring Brand Equity across Products and Markets. *California Management Review*, Vol. 38, No. 3, 102–120.

Abboud, L. and Auchard, E., 2014. *WhatsApp to Add Voice Calls after Facebook Acquisition.* Available from: http://www.reuters.com/article/2014/02/24/us-mobile-world-whatsapp-idUSBREA1N0PT20140224 [March 3, 2014].

American Association of Advertising Agencies, 2007. *How Many Advertisements is a Person Exposed to in a Day?* Available from: https://ams.aaaa.org/eweb/upload/faqs/adexposures.pdf [June 19, 2014].

Aparicio, L., 2013. *Rato pide a las familias que saneen sus deudas mientras la vivienda sube el 19%.* Available from: http://elpais.com/diario/2003/07/02/economia/1057096803_850215.html [June 12, 2014].

Apple Financial Reports 2011–2014. Available from: http://investor.apple.com/financials.cfm [May 12, 2014].

Apple Press Info 2007–2014. Available from: https://www.apple.com/pr/library/ [May 12, 2014].

Apple Financial Report 1Q14 2014. Available from: http://www.apple.com/pr/library/2014/01/27Apple-Reports-First-Quarter-Results.html [May 11, 2014].

Appleinsider, 2006. *Apple's Jobs says Michael Dell Should Eat His Own Words.* Available from: http://appleinsider.com/articles/06/01/16/apples_jobs_says_michael_dell_should_eat_his_own_words [February 3, 2014].

Así se entrenó Messi para ser un especialista en tiros libres, 2012. Available from: http://tn.com.ar/deportes/after-play/asi-se-entreno-messi-para-ser-un-especialista-en-tiros-libre_276825 [May 2, 2014].

Back to the Future Power Laces a Reality, 2014. Available from: http://www.news.com.au/technology/great-scott-back-to-the-future-power-laces-coming-in-2015/story-e6frfrnr-1226829222701 [June 16, 2014].

Bloomberg Businessweek, 2014a. *Inditex Financial Statements.* Available from: http://investing.businessweek.com/research/stocks/financials/financials.asp?ticker=ITX:SM [February 3, 2014].

Bloomberg Businessweek, 2014b. *Prada SPA Financial Statements.* Available from: http://investing.businessweek.com/research/stocks/financials/financials.asp?ticker=1913:HK [February 3, 2014].

Bloomberg Businessweek, 2014c. *Hennes & Mauritz Ab-B ShS Financial Statements.* Available from: http://investing.businessweek.com/research/stocks/financials/financials.asp?ticker=HMB:SS [February 3, 2014].

Bloomberg Businessweek, 2014d. *The Gap Inc Financial Statements.* Available from: http://investing.businessweek.com/research/stocks/financials/financials.asp?ticker=GPS [February 3, 2014].

Bloomberg Businessweek, 2014e. *La-Z-Boy Inc Financial Statements.* Available from: http://investing.businessweek.com/research/stocks/snapshot/snapshot.asp?ticker=LZB [February 3, 2014].

Bloomberg Businessweek, 2014f. *Home Depot Inc Financial Statements.* Available from: http://investing.businessweek.com/research/stocks/snapshot/snapshot.asp?ticker=HD [February 3, 2014].

Bloomberg Businessweek, 2014g. *Nike Inc Financial Statements.* Available from: http://investing.businessweek.com/research/stocks/financials/financials.asp?ticker=NKE [February 16, 2014].

Bloomberg Businessweek, 2014h. *Adidas AG Financial Statements.* Available from: http://investing.businessweek.com/research/stocks/snapshot/snapshot.asp?ticker=ADS:GR [February 16, 2014].

Bloomberg Businessweek, 2014i. *PUMA SE Financial Statements.* Available from: http://investing.businessweek.com/research/stocks/financials/financials.asp?ticker=PUM:GR [February 16, 2014].

Bureau of Labour Statistics, 2010. *2010 Bureau of Labor Statistics Consumer Expenditure Survey.* Available at: http://www.bls.gov/cex/ [March 3, 2014].

Carroll, L., 1865. *Alice's Adventures in Wonderland, and Through the Looking-Glass*, MacMillan, Chapter 6.

Cheng, A., 2014. Nike was awarded 540 patents in 2013: Here's what that means for investors. *Marketwatch.* Available from: http://blogs.marketwatch.com/behindthestorefront/2014/04/17/nike-was-awarded-540-patents-in-2013-heres-what-that-means-for-investors/ [May 10, 2014].

Coldewey, D., 2014. *WhatsApp? What's That? And Why is it Worth $16 Billion?* Available from: http://www.nbcnews.com/tech/social-media/whatsapp-whats-why-it-worth-16-billion-n34056 [March 14, 2014].

Cyren, 2014. *Internet Threads Trend Report April 2014.* Available from: http://www.cyren.com/tl_files/downloads/CYREN-Internet-Threats-Trend-Report-2014-April.pdf?mkt_tok=3RkMMJWWfF9wsRokvq3JZKXonjHpfsX57%2B4uXKC%2FlMI%2F0ER3fOvrPUfGjI4ASspnI%2BSLDwEYGJlv6SgFQ7TBMbBn1bgNXBc%3D [June 14, 2014].

D'Aveni, R. 1994. *Hypercompetition: Managing the Dynamics of Strategic Maneuvering.* Free Press.

Dediu, H., 2013. Do ads work? The ad budgets of various companies. 4 November, 2013. *Asymco.* Available from: http://www.asymco.com/2013/11/04/do-ads-work-the-ad-budgets-of-various-companies/ [May 13, 2014].

Doran, T., 1981. There's a S.M.A.R.T. way to write management's goals and objectives, *Management Review*, Vol. 70, No. 11, 35–6.

Euromonitor International, 2013. *Ikea Presence Secures Revenues but Not Market Share*. Available from: http://euromonitor.typepad.com/files/pdf_ikea-v1.0.pdf [March 3, 2014].

Fageda, X., Jiménez, J., and Perdiguero, J., 2010. Price Rivalry in Airline Markets: A Study of a Successful Strategy of a Network Carrier Against a Low-Cost Carrier. Research Institute of Applied Economics. Working Paper 2010/7 pag.2 Available from: http://www.ub.edu/irea/working_papers/2010/201007.pdf [October 14, 2014].

Farris, P., Bendle, N., Pfeifer, P. and Reibstein, D., 2006. *50+ Metrics Every Executive Should Master*. Wharton School Publishing.

Fiegerman, S., 2012. *The Biggest Apple Secrets Revealed During the First Week of the Patent Trial*. Available from: http://www.businessinsider.com/10-apple-secrets-revealed-during-the-first-week-of-the-patent-trial-2012-8?op=1#ixzz 36M5NFLvy [May 14, 2014].

Fleet Data, 2012. Available from: http://www.fleet-global.com/ [May 2, 2014].

Garvin, D.A., 1987. Competing on the Eight Dimensions of Quality, Vol. 65, No. 6, (November–December).

Go, R., 2011. Available from: http://www.businessinsider.com/we-believe-that-were-on-the-face-of-the-earth-to-make-great-products-and-thats-not-2011-1 [February 2, 2014].

Gupta, S., Hanssens, D., Hardle, B., Kahn, W., Kumar, V., Lin, N., and Siriam, N.R. 2006. Modeling Customer Lifetime Value. *Journal of Service Research,* Vol. 9, No. 2, pp. 139–55.

Hayes, R. and Wheelwright, S., 1984. *Restoring our Competitive Edge: Competing Through Manufacturing*, John Wiley & Sons.

IHS Technology, 2009. *iPhone 3G S Carries $178.96 BOM and Manufacturing Cost, iSuppli Teardown Reveals*. Available from: https://technology.ihs.com/389273/iphone-3g-s-carries-17896-bom-and-manufacturing-cost-isuppli-teardown-reveals [May 12, 2014].

IHS Technology, 2013. *Groundbreaking iPhone 5s Carries $199 BOM and Manufacturing Cost, IHS Teardown Reveals*. Available from: https://technology.ihs.com/451425/groundbreaking-iphone-5s-carries-199-bom-and-manufacturing-cost-ihs-teardown-reveals [May 12, 2014].

IKEA Yearly Summary 2010–2013. Available from: http://www.ikea.com/ms/en_JP/this-is-ikea/reports-downloads/index.html [February 3, 2014].

Inofon Mobile Phones Guide 2013. *Nokia Phones*. Available from: http://inofon.com/Nokia_phones_pr3.aspx [May 11, 2014].

Joint Research Center. 2013. Directorate-General for Research and Innovation. *EU R&D Scoreboard 2012, The 2012 EU Industrial R&D Investment Scoreboard*. European Commission. Institute for Prospective Technological Studies (2013). Available from http://iri.jrc.ec.europa.eu/scoreboard12.html [Accessed May 10, 2014].

Kim, W. Chan and Mauborgne, R., 2005. *Blue Ocean Strategy: How to Create Uncontested Market Space and Make the Competition Irrelevant,* Harvard Business Review Press.

Lego Group Annual Reports 2002–2004. Available from: http://aboutus.lego.com/en-us/lego-group/annual-report [April 8, 2014].

List of iOS devices, n.d. *Wikipedia*. Wiki article. Available from: http://en.wikipedia.org/wiki/List_of_iOS_devices#iPhone [May 12, 2014].

McKinsey & Company, 2012. *Global Media Report 2013*. Available from: http://www.mckinsey.com/~/media/mckinsey/dotcom/client_service/Media%20and%20Entertainment/PDFs/Global_Media_Report_2013.ashx [June 12, 2014].

Navigant Research, 2013. *Carsharing Membership and Vehicle Fleets, Personal Vehicle Reduction, and Revenue from Carsharing Services: Global Market Analysis and Forecasts*. Available from: http://www.navigantresearch.com/research/carsharing-programs [May 10, 2014].

Nokia Group Annual Reports 2007–2012. Available from: http://company.nokia.com/en/investors/financial-reports/results-reports [May 12, 2014].

Nostrum, 2013. Available from: http://www.nostrum.eu/en [March 14, 2014].

Patents by Assignee Puma AG Rudolf Dassler Sport, n.d. Available from: http://patents.justia.com/assignee/puma-ag-rudolf-dassler-sport?page=2 [April 3, 2014].

Porter, M., 1979. How Competitive Forces Shape Strategy. *Harvard Business Review*, March–April, pp. 137–45.

Porter, M.E., 1980. *Competitive Strategy: Techniques for Analyzing Industries and Competitors*, Free Press (Republished with a new introduction, 1998).

RAC, 2010. *RAC Cost of Motoring Index 2010*. Available from: http://www.rac.co.uk/RAC/files/e4/e4c1fe2a-5960-4bf1-9dc3-83bd314dfa54.pdf [March 3, 2014].

Rodrigue, J.P., 2008. *Rodrigue's Stages of a Bubble*. Available from http://canadianfinanceblog.com/is-the-current-market-a-return-to-normal/ [June 10, 2014].

Rocha, M., n.d. *Brand Valuation: A Versatile Strategic Tool for Business*. Available from: http://interbrand.com/Libraries/Articles/Brand_Valuation_Final.sflb.ashx [April 1, 2014].

Sociedad de Tasación, 2013. Available from: http://web.st-tasacion.es/es/inicio.html [March 17, 2014].

Shaheen, S. and Cohen A., 2012. Carsharing and Personal Vehicle Services: Worldwide Market Developments and Emerging Trends. *International Journal of Sustainable Transportation*, Vol. 7, No. 1, 5–34.

Srinivasan, S. and Hanssens, D.M., 2009. Marketing and Firm Value: Metrics, Methods, Findings, and Future Directions. *Journal of Marketing Research,* Vol. 46, pp. 293–312.

Statista, 2012. *Manufacturing Cost of the Apple iPhone 5 as of September 2012, by GB Storage*. Available from: Statista [May 13, 2014].

Surfing Australia Annual Report, 2011. Available from: http://www.surfingaustralia.com/documents/annual%20report%20-%2010-11.pdf [May 8, 2014].

Todos Los Goles de Messi, 2013. Available from: http://canchallena.lanacion.com.ar/1612284-lionel-messi-llego-a-los-350-goles-y-ya-se-fija-nuevos-records [August 20, 2013].

'WhatsApp' n.d. *Wikipedia*. Wiki article. Available from: http://en.wikipedia.org/wiki/WhatsApp [May 11, 2014].

Winters, L.C. 1991. Brand Equity Measures: Some Recent Advances. *Marketing Research*, Vol. 3, No, 4, pp. 70–72.

Ycharts, 2013. Avaialable from: http://ycharts.com/ [April 2, 2014].

'Zipcar' n.d. *Wikipedia*. Wiki article. Available from: http://en.wikipedia.org/wiki/Zipcar [May 4, 2014].

Zipcar Reports 2010–2012. Available from: http://www.zipcar.com/press/releases/zipcar-reports-2011-full-results [May 4, 2014].

INDEX